The

Rutgers Films in Print

Mirella Jona Affron, Robert Lyons,
and E. Rubinstein, editors

My Darling Clementine, John Ford, director
edited by Robert Lyons

The Last Metro, François Truffaut, director
edited by Mirella Jona Affron and
E. Rubinstein

The Last Metro

François Truffaut, director

Mirella Jona Affron and

E. Rubinstein, editors

Rutgers University Press

New Brunswick, New Jersey

Library of Congress Cataloging in
Publication Data
Main entry under title:
The Last metro.

(Rutgers films in print; v. 2)
Bibliography: p.
I. Affron, Mirella Jona,
1937- . II. Rubinstein, E. (Elliot),
1936- . III. Dernier métro. IV. Series.
PN1997.D453 1985   791.43′72   84–9838
ISBN 0–8135–1065–1
ISBN 0–8135–1066–X (pbk.)

Contents

The Last Metro

Introduction

The Last Metro
and the Cinema of
the Occupation

Mirella Jona Affron

François Truffaut's realization of *The Last Metro* fulfilled a desire nurtured since his elaboration of the script of *The 400 Blows* in 1958: to make a film that evokes the atmosphere of the Occupation. Truffaut recalled that at that early point in his career he had wanted the adventures of young Antoine Doinel to be served by "a thousand details of [his] adolescence that were tied to the period of the Occupation, but the [film's] budget and the spirit of the 'New Wave' were not compatible with the notion of a 'period film.'"[1] Ten years passed. Truffaut's desire to make a film about the Occupation persisted and, in 1968, he was again tempted to reconstruct the era of German rule. He "was stopped in [his] tracks," not by budget or by New Wave dogma this time, but "by a remarkable film: Marcel Ophuls's *The Sorrow and the Pity*."[2] Nearly ten more years went by as Truffaut continued to search for his solution to the stylistic problems attendant upon a rendering of life in occupied France during the Second World War. He noted: "A film on the Occupation should take place almost entirely at night and in enclosed spaces; it should reconstruct the period through darkness, claustration, frustration, and danger, and, as the sole luminous element, it should include, in their original recordings, some of the songs that were heard at the time in the streets and on the radio."[3] In the end, however, it was Truffaut's

---

1. François Truffaut, "Pourquoi et comment Le Dernier métro?" *L'Avant-Scène Cinéma*, nos. 303–4 (1–15 March 1983), p. 4. Translation mine.
2. Ibid., p. 4.
3. Ibid., pp. 4–5.

rediscovery of the cinema of the period that provided the inspiration for his film about Paris during the Occupation.

The period 1939–1944 coincides with Truffaut's own formative years. In 1939 hostilities began between France and Germany; it is also the year in which Truffaut, age seven, saw the film that was to provide him with his first indelible screen memory, Abel Gance's *Paradise Lost* (*Paradis perdu*), a depiction of the French experience in the trenches and on the home front during the Great War. In 1942, at the height of the German occupation of Paris, Truffaut, age ten, adopted the practice that was to mark him most profoundly: he began to frequent the movies obsessively and clandestinely. In 1944, just before the Liberation, the twelve-year-old Truffaut, already a formidable spectator-collector, often fled from the reality of the German presence to the enormous Gaumont-Palace, where a friend's mother held the privileged position of ticket-taker.

Some five years before *The Last Metro*, Truffaut was engaged in preparing a volume of the 1943–1945 notices and essays of his mentor, André Bazin, one of cinema's most original and influential critics.[4] The Bazin volume led Truffaut back to the political and moral climate of the French cinema of the early forties, those years of war, defeat, and occupation, of Vichy and Pétain, of collaboration, survival, resistance, and finally of liberation. To provide a context for his collection of Bazin's early work, Truffaut consulted contemporary documents and the memoirs of fellow artists. Equally important was the filter of Truffaut's own memory of that time and the perspective gained over the intervening thirty years. The original French version, called *The Cinema of the Occupation and Resistance*, appeared in 1975. Five years later, a work of scholarship was to inspire a work of the imagination: *The Last Metro*.

Truffaut introduces the Bazin collection with an essay that announces the spirit, and even the plot, of the film that was to follow. In this preface he describes the role of the cinema and the theater in the lives of the citizens of occupied Paris and the sanctuary theaters provided a deprived population until the day the Germans began to scour entrances and exits for recruits for their labor camps. He evokes the air-raid sirens that interrupted performances and the air-raid shelters that offered safety to audiences reluctant to leave their seats. He recalls the blacking out of Jewish names on screen credits and anti-Semitic re-

---

4. The English-language edition is André Bazin, *French Cinema of the Occupation and Resistance: The Birth of a Critical Esthetic*, ed. François Truffaut, trans. Stanley Hochman (New York: Frederick Ungar, 1981).

views in the pro-Fascist newspaper, *Je suis partout* (I Am Everywhere). He reminisces about an aunt who, through a friend employed at the cosmetics counter of a large department store, was able to put her hands on a prohibited and most precious prize—a copy of the banned *Gone with the Wind*. And finally he recalls the very slow diction of the actor Alain Cuny ("the grass grows between his lines," said one critic) that delayed the final curtain until audiences found themselves in danger of being caught on the streets after curfew, having missed the last metro.

These and many other references, based on the facts of everyday life in Paris during the Occupation as well as on personal, even nostalgic recollection, have a strong presence in *The Last Metro*. The film's Théâtre Montmartre is indeed a haven, not only for Lucas Steiner hidden in its cellar, but for the players and theater-goers for whom the few hours of performance each evening are an escape from the humiliating realities of the Occupation. One member of the company, Bernard Granger, tells of an actor's trick that he used to elude the recruiters for forced labor camps posted outside a movie house. Toward the end of the film, Gestapo agents, suspicious that Steiner may never have left the theater, conduct a mock inspection of the cellar for use as an air raid shelter. Daxiat, the anti-Semitic critic, is closely modeled on Alain Laubreaux, the reviewer for *Je suis partout* during the Occupation years. Securing a copy of *Gone with the Wind* for Marion Steiner—through a contact of Martine's employed at the Galeries Lafayette—is borrowed directly from Truffaut's memory of his aunt. And whether because of the slow pace of an actor, or for other reasons, the fear of missing the last metro, one of the very real terrors of the Occupation, gives the film its title.

At the beginning of his introduction to *The Cinema of the Occupation and Resistance*, Truffaut notes that Bazin's reviews and essays of the Occupation years illuminate but do not judge the period in question. Criticism with a political or moral point of view would have to await the Liberation. Even then it remained cautious, presumably to safeguard the national honor. Not until the death of General de Gaulle (1970) and the appearance of Marcel Ophuls's documentary, *The Sorrow and the Pity* (*Le Chagrin et la pitié*, 1971), did the question of French collaboration with the Nazis during the Occupation undergo public examination. Only then were official versions, often simplistic, invariably distorted, contested in national debate.

Ophuls's film may well be better remembered for prompting newspaper and television inquiry into French collaboration than for the place it commands in film history. *The Sorrow and the Pity* was a Swiss and German co-production. Lasting more than three hours, and subtitled "Chronicle of a French City under the Occupation," it is composed essentially of documentary footage of the time and of interviews with persons who had witnessed the events depicted and discussed: political leaders, local officials, peasants, shopkeepers, aristocrats, collaborators, resisters, survivors, heroes, and cowards. Jacques Siclier notes in his study of French film during the Vichy years:

> The official version of a France united in Resistance against Germany and a handful of collaborators (to which the cinema up to that point had subscribed) collapsed all at once. The reality of France under the Vichy regime was revealed in all its ambiguity, shadiness, cowardice, moral decomposition, as well as with its legitimate share of resistance. The generation that had just shaped the events of May 1968 discovered the truth previously hidden under the mask of the version imposed.[5]

The French government-controlled television (ORTF) declined the rights to the broadcast of *The Sorrow and the Pity*, hoping to avoid through simple neglect the challenge the film posed to its official position. Showings in movie theaters provoked impassioned controversy, however, and the ORTF's refusal to air the film, judged to be a form of censorship, added further fuel to the polemic.

Since *The Sorrow and the Pity*, a number of filmmakers have treated the theme of French collaboration with fascism during the war. Prominent among them are Costa Gavras (*Special Section*, 1974), Louis Malle (*Lacombe Lucien*, 1974), and Joseph Losey (*Mr. Klein*, 1976). Yet, the influence of Ophuls's example on these and other works is difficult to calculate, so varying are they in style and degree of candor. And although the proportion of films on the Occupation before *The Sorrow and the Pity* is small in relation to the total output of the French film industry for that period, the fact remains that in almost every year between 1944 and 1971, one or more such films was produced. Of these, however, not more than a handful are of note.

The very first, and still one of the most celebrated, was *The Liberation of Paris*, sponsored by the Committee on the Liberation of French Cinema in anticipation of the uprising of the capital and begun just as the Allies were approaching the city. *The Liberation of Paris* was first shown on August 24, 1944, in the open,

---

5. Jacques Siclier, *La France de Pétain et son cinéma* (Paris: Henri Veyrier, 1981), pp. 251–52. Translation mine.

on a giant screen, just days and hours after the events photographed. In that same year, René Clément directed *The Battle of the Rails*, whose subject is the clandestine war waged by French railroad workers against the Germans. (Twenty-two years later, in 1966, Clément directed *Is Paris Burning?*, similar in subject to *The Liberation of Paris*, although opposed in style. Based on a best-seller, *Is Paris Burning?* was, alone among the films on the war years in France, an international production on a grand scale.) In 1947, Jean-Pierre Melville made his first film, *Le Silence de la mer*, adapted from Vercors's story of the stony reception accorded a well-intentioned German officer billeted in a French home. The next year, Henri-Georges Clouzot made a modern version of the eighteenth-century novel *Manon Lescaut*, in which he depicts the insidious corruption of French black-marketeers. René Clément's *Forbidden Games* (1951), perhaps the best known of the films about the period, begins with an account of the exodus of refugees after the French defeat in the North. The forbidden games of the title are the burial rites performed on dead animals by two children caught in the trauma of the war.

Nineteen fifty-five saw the first film on the war years made by one of the New Wave era directors: Alain Resnais's documentary of concentration camps, *Night and Fog*. Resnais's first feature film, *Hiroshima, mon amour* (1959), is in part at least the story of an obsessive memory born in the town of Nevers during the Occupation: the first love of a young woman for a German soldier, her punishment for fraternizing with the enemy, her disgrace and her eventual banishment. Claude Chabrol, another of the first generation New Wave directors, followed some years later with a melodramatic tale of resistance at the boundary between Vichy and occupied France, *Line of Demarcation* (1966). And—in this case working after Ophuls's film—yet another New Wave director, Malle in *Lacombe Lucien*, recounted the adventures of a typically anti-Semitic French peasant who attempts, futilely as it turns out, to save a Jewish girl.

Well before *The Last Metro*, then, many of the prominent New Wave directors of Truffaut's generation (the most obvious exceptions are Godard and Rivette), had made films about France during the war years. The sensibilities and style evident in their treatments of this subject reflect the differences that distinguish Resnais, Chabrol, Malle, and Truffaut. They converge at many points, nonetheless, initially, of course, in their admiration for two French masters of preceding generations who shared the commitment to personal cinema known as auteurism: Jean Renoir and Robert Bresson. Even before 1958 when the young

Cahiers du cinéma critics—who would become the New Wave directors—began making their own films, both Renoir and Bresson had given their accounts of France under German rule.

Renoir's *This Land Is Mine* (1943) was one of the five feature films the director made in Hollywood, where he took refuge from the Nazis in 1941. *This Land Is Mine* starred Charles Laughton as the cowardly schoolmaster of an occupied French town who, in a final patriotic gesture, sacrifices his life to his honor and his country. *This Land Is Mine*, despite the marked influence of the Hollywood studio style, retains the imprint of Renoir's characteristic themes and compositions. To his lasting chagrin, Renoir was attacked almost universally in the French press at the film's release in Europe after the war. He was accused of failing to understand the realities of survival under Nazi domination.

Bresson's film *A Man Escaped* (*Un Condamné à mort s'est échappé*, 1956) is based on the autobiographical account of a French officer who managed a daring escape from the dreaded prison of Lyons. Nazis and collaborators hardly appear in *A Man Escaped*. The viewer is confined with the hero to a cell, and only occasionally allowed a walk through the prison corridors or yard. As one has come to expect of Bresson, it is the officer's consciousness, along with his ineluctable fate, rather than particular circumstances of war, occupation, or resistance, that determines the action of the film.

Truffaut, like his cherished models Renoir and Bresson, made *his* film about France during the Occupation. Like Bresson's, *The Last Metro* reflects the obsessions of the director rather than larger historical or ideological issues; like Renoir's, it bears the stamp of a characteristic mise-en-scène; and like Bazin's reviews collected in *The Cinema of the Occupation and Resistance*, it casts more light than judgment on the period in question.

Chronology of
Political Events
France, 1939–1944

Winter, 1939–1940   France and Germany are at war. This is the period known as the "phony war" or *drôle de guerre*.

May 1940   The German army breaks through the French lines and begins its invasion of France.

June 10, 1940   The German army meets no resistance in occupying Paris; the French government leaves Paris for Bordeaux.

June 16, 1940   The French cabinet votes to request armistice terms. It is recommended that Marshal Pétain be appointed premier.

June 18, 1940   General Charles de Gaulle, who had fled from Bordeaux to London, issues a call for continued resistance and sets up the Free French movement.

June 22, 1940   The surrender is signed in the railroad car that had served as the site of the German capitulation to France in 1918. Pending a final peace settlement, two-thirds of France (the area north of the Loire Valley and all of the Atlantic Coast) was to be occupied by German troops.

July 1, 1940   The new French government is installed at Vichy, a city in the nonoccupied zone, located near the line of demarcation.

July 10, 1940	Pétain is vested with full powers by a 569 to 80 vote of parliament. The period of collaboration begins.
1940–1944	Underground movements of resistance are organized in the German-occupied North and in the unoccupied southern zone. In 1943, de Gaulle's agents in France organize the underground movements into a nation-wide federation, the National Resistance Council. The underground paramilitary forces are also united under a single command, the French Forces of the Interior (FFI).
1942–1944	With the consent of the Vichy government, French workers are conscripted into service in Germany; foreign-born Jews are turned over to the Germans in return for the promise to spare French Jews; a special corps of French police and special courts are empowered to arrest and punish "terrorists"; French men and women are deported to concentration camps in large numbers.
November 1942	The Allies land in North Africa; the Germans occupy all of France. De Gaulle transfers his headquarters from London to Algiers.
June 6, 1944	D Day. Allied troops land in Normandy. Liberated territories are turned over to de Gaulle's representatives.
August 25, 1944	Paris is liberated. De Gaulle makes his triumphal entry, flanked by members of the National Resistance Council. The last holdouts of Vichy are hunted down.

The Last Metro
and the
Preoccupations
of Cinema

E. Rubinstein

In a career spanning over twenty years and encompassing eighteen feature films up to the time of *The Last Metro*, François Truffaut made only a handful of period pieces, but at least three of these must number among his major achievements. For Truffaut, "period" was not, as in so many historical films, merely a pretext for interesting or flattering costumes and for sumptuous architectural reproduction. What interested Truffaut was the particular forms imposed by history on human feeling; he illuminated (in all his work, but perhaps most vividly in the period films) the specific limited options that any moment of history opens up to human will and the limited range of social styles in which at any given historical moment we are free to clothe and dramatize ourselves.

In *The Wild Child* (1969), for example, a film set at the very beginning of the nineteenth century, the conflict between the "civilized" teacher and the "primitive" foundling who must be reborn into human society—into one particular human society—is presented as the final chapter in the history of eighteenth-century philosophy and pedagogics, with all the opposing forces of that story (human art versus human nature, the weight of culture versus the power of impulse, the nobility versus the savagery in the figure of the "noble savage") set in full operation. *The Story of Adele H.* (1975)—the story, that is, of the mad daughter of Victor Hugo, most prodigious and renowned of the Romantic French writers—demonstrates the forms that madness may assume not only in the family of an awesome father but in a world controlled by the Romantic imagination. (Both *The Wild Child* and *Adele H.*, by the way, are based on actual autobiographical documents.) In *Jules and Jim* (1961), Truffaut's subject is the un-settled, anarchic, artistically fertile period from the time just before World War I to the rise of Hitler; its characters are obsessed not only with one another but with books (the sort of books Hitler burns at the end of the film), with the precarious border area between life and art, with various assertions of personal freedom in the face of a doom as unimaginable as it was inevitable.

At roughly the moment when the narrative of *Jules and Jim* ends, François Truffaut was born. The recreation of the world of *Jules and Jim* was therefore for Truffaut as much an act of historical imagination as the recreation of the far more distant worlds of *The Wild Child* and *Adele H.* Not until *The Last Metro* would Truffaut confront the challenge of interpreting a period of his own lifetime that had passed into history—a period which, moreover, would lie as completely outside the actual memory of much of the movie public of 1980 as the period of *Jules and Jim* lay outside Truffaut's memory. The job Truffaut took upon himself could only have been complicated by the fact that the years of the Nazi occupa-tion of Paris were not merely a few years in Truffaut's life but among the most nearly crucial of his or anyone's life, the years of late childhood and early adoles-cence. And the job was further complicated by the fact that a directly autobio-graphical approach was presumably ruled out by Truffaut's already having dramatized this period of his life in *The 400 Blows* (1959). There, because of financial restrictions and New Wave aesthetics, he was obliged to eschew the autobiographically accurate period setting of the Occupation. Indeed, however otherwise accurate their allusions to Truffaut's life, *all* the Antoine Doinel films (see "François Truffaut; A Biographical Sketch" below) are, as autobiography, imprecise in terms of historical period: to maintain continuity with the world of *The 400 Blows*, Truffaut was obliged again and again to rephrase his own life in terms of contemporary dress and settings, and, most important of all, contempo-rary manners. A considerable part of Truffaut's oeuvre, the autobiographical line—perhaps the most substantial body of autobiographical work any filmmaker has left us—is built on a false historical scaffolding; given Truffaut's historical sense, this must have been for him the most serious of all the departures from "truth" in the Antoine Doinel films.

In any event, in *The Last Metro* there is no single figure whom one might simply identify with Truffaut. (Little Jacquot, the only character whose age is even close to that of Truffaut during the Occupation, is too sketchily drawn to sustain the weight of authorial identification.) Truffaut's strategy for suggesting a child's point of view is more subtle. Drawing upon the naturally secretive and indirect modes that behavior will take under an oppressive foreign domination that encourages and rewards spying and informing, he presents the viewer with a situation in which the characters' actions *must* seem inconsistent and puzzling and in which the characters' motives *must* seem hopelessly unfathomable: what better way to dramatize the way the adult world is so often perceived by alert, inquisitive children?

True, to the extent that we penetrate the world of *The Last Metro* through the discoveries of the young actor Bernard Granger (Gérard Depardieu), Bernard determines our narrative viewpoint. Bernard notices from the start that there is something not quite right about Marion Steiner (Catherine Deneuve), but he is hardly prepared for the chilling revelation that she has secreted her Jewish husband in the cellar of their theater. Smaller surprises attend Bernard (and the viewer) at every turn: some are comprehensible once disclosed, such as the designer Arlette's lesbianism (along with the apparently unlimited range of compliances of the fiercely ambitious young actress Nadine); some, like the physical violence of Marion's reaction when Bernard tells her he is leaving the theater for the Resistance, only deepen the mystery. But despite all this, Bernard does not provide the audience with a fixed viewpoint. We find out about Lucas Steiner (Heinz Bennent) in the cellar long, long before Bernard: for much of the film we observe, but do not share, his ignorance of Marion's purposes. Moreover, Bernard himself is capable of behavior that the audience cannot adequately interpret: when we see him fussing backstage with a phonograph, we have no clear idea, we can at best dimly suspect, that the machine will figure in a major Resistance action. No: for all the backstage camaraderie at the Théâtre Montmartre, everyone in *The Last Metro* at least *seems* to harbor undisclosed motives. That is life under Nazi surveillance. And that is life as a child might see it.

The illegibility of surfaces, the multifariousness of indirection and deception—one might identify these as the controlling themes of *The Last Metro*. In casting the film and constructing its scenario, Truffaut came up with at least two very nearly ideal visual correlatives of these themes. The first is the face of Catherine Deneuve. Confronted with the mask of sovereign, indecipherable beauty that Deneuve presents to the world, one is obliged to read her as an avatar of mystery. In *The Last Metro*'s original French pressbook, Truffaut states that in this film he wished to give Deneuve the chance to play a "woman of responsibility"; he might have added that his alertness to Deneuve's particular appeal as a screen presence required not only that he keep the actual scope of her "responsibility" hidden from the other characters in the film (except, of course, from her husband), but that he never allow her to disclose fully, not even to her husband and not even to the viewer of the film, the true register of her feelings. Again and again, Truffaut brings the camera close to that face so as to suggest, but never to reveal, the affective mysteries that will transcend any and all specific puzzles of the plot and that will remain unresolved in the viewer's mind to the very last frames of the film, where Deneuve, flanked by her husband and her lover as all three receive an ovation from the Théâtre Montmartre audience, grants us a bewitching smile. In this regard too, one must add, Truffaut impresses on us a childlike point of view: in Deneuve's face he locates the source of a romantic boy's wonder at the beauty *and* the incomprehensibility of this ideal adult woman.

Truffaut's other principal visual device is the playhouse itself. Only rarely does Truffaut move the action outside the Théâtre Montmartre and its immediate environs; this playhouse, he persuades us, is a very nearly self-sustaining organism. With its stage and its auditorium, its kitchens and bathrooms and business offices, its marital bed and chambers of assignation, the theater accommodates both the everyday activities and the complex emotional transactions of life. But what haunts the viewer's memory—perhaps more vividly even than the faces and gestures of the principal characters—is the corridors and stairways and trapdoors and unanticipated exitways: if this is a world, it is, more specifically, a world of sudden appearances and of stealthy escapes. Annette Insdorf takes the point further:

> One way to read the film is in terms of displacement: we constantly see characters being moved around, not only onstage but up and down the stairs: Bernard refuses to take the place of Rosen, the Jewish actor with Aryan papers; and we don't really see anti-Semitism as much as French individuals who want for themselves the desirable situations occupied by Jews. . . .
> The Nazi impulse in Paris is depicted in terms of expulsion—"France is off-limit to Jews," declares Daxiat on the radio—or loss of place. More specifically, it is symbolized by Lucas being forced off his stage into placelessness—a room as self-enclosed as a stage.[1]

Thinking always in cinematic terms, Truffaut translates his themes into spatial arrangements and spatial dislocations, and he shapes and orders his vision by remaining largely within the physical boundaries of a single playhouse.

1. Annette Insdorf, *Indelible Shadows: Film and the Holocaust* (New York: Vintage Books, 1983), p. 87.

Moreover, the visual "symbol" of Lucas's displacement permits Truffaut to explore still further implications of the narrative. Carefully listening both to the rehearsals of the play in production and to the emotional reverberations of his wife's onstage but unscripted interchanges with Bernard, Lucas must remain the auditor, in permanent exile from the principal business of the theater. In Lucas Steiner, then, Truffaut suggests not only the frustrations of a child who may not assert himself in the world of adult drama and adult competition but also the frustrations of the director whose actual contributions to the finished performance will never be fully known and acknowledged. Again, one cannot speak of simple identification of author and character (as one can more reasonably speak of such identification, however ironic, in *Day for Night* [1973], where Truffaut himself plays the role of the director—a film and not a stage director). The autobiographical elements in *The Last Metro* are only suggestions, threads woven into the film's fabric so subtly that they never stand out as one plainly marked pattern but without which the fabric would be recognizably different.

But Truffaut's most telling method of asserting his own presence in *The Last Metro*, of locating his own imagination and memory in the world of the film, is not the muted autobiographical echoes nor the pervasive sense of unfathomable adult mystery, but rather the sheer density of allusion to other films.

Near the end of the film—the time, the voice-over narration tells us, is the late summer of 1944—we see Deneuve enter a crowded hospital ward in search of Depardieu. She finds him—immobilized, in a wheelchair. We are saddened but not surprised to see him so grievously crippled, for we knew that he had determined to spend the last period of the Occupation fighting in the Resistance. The conversation we now hear, like Depardieu's condition, makes sense in the narrative context the film has established. Despite her attraction to Depardieu, Deneuve's first commitment had always been to her husband. But in this scene we learn that Lucas Steiner—here called only "he"—is dead; we know that the war is, at least for the French, effectively over; Deneuve's work as manager pro tem and star of her husband's theater, she claims, has ceased to interest her; she finds herself at last able to give herself to her lover. But Depardieu claims that his own passion for Deneuve—surely at least in part the response of a young actor to a great lady of legendary, timeless beauty—was only what he now calls an "abstraction." Even so, his rejection of the love she proffers seems inexplicably cold, even rehearsed. Is he protecting her from devoting her life once again to a man who cannot fully be her husband—from transferring her commitment from a prisoner to a cripple? Deneuve's departure from this interview is colored by deep ambiguities; assuring Depardieu that she will love him in spite of himself, she nonetheless exits on the apparent finality of an "adieu." Upon her departure, Depardieu thaws somewhat; he lifts his hands to cover his face. So, in uncertainty and despair, ends the primary narrative of *The Last Metro*, the story of lives confined and confused and marooned and destroyed by war.

But wait. As Depardieu sinks into his solitary grief, stage curtains are suddenly drawn closed before him. He rises from his wheelchair and walks downstage, ready to receive the homage of an enthusiastic audience. Deneuve joins him to acknowledge the applause. And so does her husband, the play's director, not only still alive but apparently none the worse for the long ordeal of his incarceration. The scene in the hospital has been no more than a scene in a play. Though this kind of trick substitution of stage for life is a device that filmmakers have played with at least since Hitchcock's *Murder!* (1930), seldom has it been utilized with such scrupulousness. The hospital set, for instance, seemed, as Deneuve entered it and took her place beside Depardieu, a "realistic" one, no challenge to our sense that the episode was to continue the film's central narrative. Past the windows of the ward we watched human figures stirring. But during the dialogue between Deneuve and Depardieu, Truffaut has—uncharacteristically for him in this film—blurred the background; as Deneuve prepares to depart and the camera pulls back, the background—the courtyard, the two sets of windows—is once more in focus, but now transformed into a painted theater flat. Suddenly we are free to admit that, however dramatically logical in the narrative of *The Last Metro*, the dialogue has struck our ears as totally wanting in vitality or invention. Thanks to the fact that we were so taken in by Truffaut's ruse, we realize too that the hospital scene has been inserted not only as a way of delaying, and so of intensifying the actual happy resolution of the film, but as a device for reminding us how things *might* have gone in those grim years of the early 1940s—for reminding us that, as in any fictional narrative, alternative endings are always available, and the happiest at least as arbitrary as the most doleful.

But wait. This image of a man at the end of a film rising unexpectedly, miraculously, from the wheelchair to which the action of the film has doomed him—have we not seen this somewhere before? And—the recognitions begin to come alive—was not Catherine Deneuve somewhere implicated in this other film? Of course: we are put in mind of the end of the great Spanish filmmaker Luis Buñuel's *Belle de Jour* (1966), where, in Buñuel's deliberate confusion, or identification, of something called "fantasy" with something called "reality" (all in the name of something called cinema), Jean Servais, paralyzed by a gunshot from his wife's gangster lover, amiably discards his paraplegia and walks toward Deneuve. Now another detail may strike us: in this sequence of *The Last Metro*, Deneuve, who had previously favored muted colors for her wardrobe, appears in an outfit of severe black and white—the color scheme of Buñuel's Séverine/ Belle de Jour. And may we not connect all this with a detail from earlier in Truffaut's film? Christian, the Resistance fighter, speaks of a notorious film that appeared at the time of his First Communion: from his appearance, we may suppose that that event took place, say, fifteen years before the present action. The film starred Marion Steiner—that is, Catherine Deneuve. It was entitled *La Maison du péché* (*The House of Sin*). Well, about fifteen years before Catherine Deneuve appeared as the star of *The Last Metro*, she did indeed appear (it remains her most famous role) in a film that might well have been called *The House of Sin*, a film about a wealthy lady driven to spend her afternoons in a house of prostitution—only Buñuel chose to name the film after the novel on which it was based, to name it not *The House of Sin* but *Belle de Jour*.

To the degree that they demonstrate Truffaut's sense that all movies operate within a context defined by other movies, a context it is part of the filmmaker's job to bring to our awareness, these allusions to *Belle de Jour* evince one of Truffaut's abiding preoccupations. Still, compared to other cinematic allusions in his work, these are both brief and somewhat muted. Not so the resounding echoes of Ernst Lubitsch's *To Be or Not to Be* (1942), a celebrated comedy about an acting troupe in Nazi-occupied Poland. Admittedly, the differences between *To Be or Not to Be* and *The Last Metro* are as palpable as the similarities: while the latter is for the most part perspicuous in its main narrative lines, the former boasts one of Lubitsch's more addling plots; where Lubitsch stresses the ways in which unimaginable horrors may frame farce, Truffaut illuminates the comic absurdities that must arise from any situation that defies individual control; where Lubitsch casts Carole Lombard, Truffaut casts Catherine Deneuve, and each filmmaker plays cannily upon the strength of his star (compare the ways in which ebullient Lombard and mysterious Deneuve are made to deal with the question of marital infidelity); and there could hardly be a place in *The Last Metro* for the likes of Lubitsch's hero, Jack Benny. But for all this, reverberations of *To Be or Not to Be*, a film that has persistently haunted Truffaut's imagination, pervade *The Last Metro*. Both films dramatize not only the desperate farcicality of world politics and the farcical desperation of playing (that is, performing plays) for time, but also the bizarre affinities between the two. Indeed, the sequence that opens *To Be or Not to Be*—a foolish scene ostensibly set in Gestapo headquarters that turns out to be a foolish scene being played out on a stage during World War II—can justly be taken as the very point of departure of *The Last Metro*.

Nor is *To Be or Not to Be* the only film about theater we recognize in *The Last Metro*. Notable among the others is Marcel Carné's *The Children of Paradise* (*Les Enfants du paradis*, 1944), a chronicle of nineteenth-century theatrical life and perhaps the best remembered of all films dealing with life on and off a particular stage. To take a small but telling illustration: the first sequence of *The Last Metro* (following the opening historical montage) shows us Depardieu attempting to pick up Andréa Ferréol on the street; as more than one reviewer observed, the sequence is a virtual recension of an early sequence in *The Children of Paradise*. (The noted French actress in *The Children of Paradise* went by the professional name of Arletty. The character played by Ferréol is called Arlette.) Moreover, the fact that *The Children of Paradise* was made in Paris during the Occupation confers upon it a special weight in the context of *The Last Metro*: for Truffaut—for the man who made *Day for Night*, the quintessential film about the procedures of filming—any drama we see enacted in any film is cognate with the various dramas that constituted the film's production.

But since Truffaut's ties—personal, cinematic, spiritual—with Jean Renoir have always been so profound, it is to Renoir that we must look for the most fertile of all Truffaut's sources. There are, first of all, the Renoir films literally concerned with theater (e.g., *The Golden Coach* [*Le Carrosse d'or*, 1953], or *French Cancan* [1955]). There are the Renoir films in which specifically theatrical elements are used either as points of ironic reference (e.g., *La Chienne* [1931], with its opening and closing puppet shows) or as integral elements of the plot (e.g., the revue in the prisoner-of-war camp in *The Grand Illusion* [1937] and the château theatricals in *The Rules of the Game* [*La Règle du jeu*, 1939]). There is, underlying all and any of these, Renoir's sense of life itself. For Renoir, society, with its small amours and great wars, is a giant arena of illusions and deceptions, accommodating the most elegant social behavior and the most monstrous lies, the most noble of impersonations and the most inept attempts at disguise; Renoir's world is an elaborate organism animated by the essentially theatrical rituals of war and friendship and love. Even more pungently than Lubitsch, Renoir repudiates the boundary between the make-believe of theater and the make-believe of life. And in *The Last Metro*, Renoir's most gifted disciple rehearses the lessons of the master. When, for example, Depardieu prepares to leave the theater for the Resistance—to abjure the petty illusions of his métier for The Grand Illusion itself—Deneuve hands him his make-up boxes. He tells her that where he now goes there is no need for "make-up." But, Deneuve suggests, there may be some need for a "disguise." And what, we are here nearly bullied into reflecting, is the real difference? Similarly, when, freed from years of imprisonment in the cellar of his own theater, the director Lucas Steiner emerges into a scene of the kind of senseless street fighting that always seems to mark the end of wars, he almost instantly begins to "direct" the action ("No, not there!" he cries to an endangered passer-by, pointing him to the correct position of safety in this "scene"). It is possible that, if Truffaut had never come under Renoir's influence, he would have become a filmmaker, and would even have made a film about the Paris theater under the Occupation. But it would not be the film we know as The Last Metro.

At the same time—and notwithstanding the words of several early reviewers who were, understandably, struck by the very evident resemblances between The Last Metro and The Golden Coach—Truffaut's vision of theater diverges significantly from Renoir's. True, like Renoir, Truffaut is happy to show the ironic affinities between forms of acting that specifically acknowledge their own theatricality and forms that do not; like Renoir, Truffaut understands the playhouse, each playhouse, as a unique little world—unique in its ethics and internal politics as well as in its physical detail; like Renoir, Truffaut (as in the "hospital" sequence discussed above) enjoys toying with the viewer's assumption that he or she can effortlessly spot the difference between on-stage and off-stage behavior. But nowhere, at least in this film, does Truffaut seem to partake of Renoir's sense of the stage itself as a sanctified or even a privileged place, as one preeminent and timeless medium of access to heights and extremes of experience otherwise unknowable to us. Nor does he see the very ritual of performance as an act in itself ennobling, an act capable of transcending even the deficiencies of taste and technique of the writing and presentation of so paltry a piece as The Vanished One, the play that consumes the energies of Deneuve and Depardieu and the others for most of the film. Naturally enough, it is Truffaut's camera that clinches the point: nowhere does the camera acknowledge the space of the stage as integral and meaningful in itself, nowhere does the camera consistently affirm the proscenium itself as a fixed frame as valid as any of the shifting frames the screen can impose. The on-stage sequences are viewed from a variety of perspectives and angles (sometimes within the same short scene), with the actors now in close range, now seen from a distance and angle suggesting the view from the balcony, and so on; the on-stage sequences, in other words, are subject to the *film* director's imagination and rarely if ever honor the emphases and valences of a *stage* director's vision. The scenes enacted on the stage of the Théâtre Montmartre are permitted to signify only as episodes in the overall drama of survival that is *The Last Metro*. Except as a demonstration of the courage and the perseverance of the troupe (and, almost incidentally, as a demonstration of the skill and invention of the set designer, Ferréol/Arlette), these scenes are, at very least, unremarkable. Would Renoir have asked us to see this theater, any theater, with such disregard for its liberating potentialities?

Truffaut's prefatory remarks to the pressbook issued in France, in which he writes, "I want to satisfy three wishes: to show the backstage of a theater, to evoke the atmosphere of the Occupation, and to cast Catherine Deneuve in the role of a woman of responsibility," are assembled under the title "Why *The Last Metro*"; significantly, and quite pointedly, Truffaut makes no mention of the theatrical experience as such.[2] And, speaking of the finished film, he states the hope that it expresses not only his and Suzanne Schiffman's "aversion to all forms of racism and intolerance" but also "our affection for those who have chosen the profession of acting and who practice that profession through thick and thin." Again, Truffaut—whose movie sets were arenas of improvisation, who generally disdained "finished" shooting scripts—honors the actor's commitment and courage without really suggesting that some honor might be due the plays that actors are called upon to perform, some affirmative notice be taken of the transcendental powers of live public performance. Truffaut's emphases and partialities are patent in *The Last Metro* itself: Deneuve and Depardieu are movie stars of 1980 working in that which Truffaut recalled, and not without considerable irony, as one prevailing theatrical mode of the 1940s; they play themselves playing actors playing out little scenes of the most glaring and mindless untruthfulness. The intrepidity of theater folk, the fascination of movie stars: these Truffaut avows, perhaps more generously than anyone else, along with demonstrating the ways the camera can help refute our perception of "theater" and "reality." The power and integrity of living theater he all but denies.

Why then indeed *The Last Metro*? To flesh out the reasons that Truffaut himself gives, one must note that aside from all else "to evoke the atmosphere of the

---

2. Elsewhere—in several interviews, for example—Truffaut does speak more fully of theater, but tends to stress the courage and indomitability of actors and the sociology of theater-going during the Occupation.

Occupation" meant, for Truffaut, not only to reanimate the atmosphere of his own youth but to externalize his own memory of Occupation movies. Truffaut's career was to a considerable extent the attempt to erase once and for all those lines supposed to delimit individual memories of a period and memories of movies made *during* that period and movies made *about* that period. (Nestor Almendros, in discussing his search for the lighting and colors suited to the film, admits the interdependence of his personal memories of the 1940s and of that shared memory called "the cinema itself"; see "Working on the Last Metro," in this volume.) Second—it is a point that I have in part already illustrated—*The Last Metro* is less "about" the theater than "about" *films* about theater—about a cinematic genre. And so the film must be about the profession of filmmaking no less than about that "profession of acting" to which Truffaut has called specific attention; and so, not surprisingly, the film will lay bare this particular filmmaker's world of cinematic associations and allusions, reminiscences and anticipations.

A few instances: (1) Deneuve plays a woman called "Marion." Hardly the most common of French given names, Marion is also the name (or one of the names) of the character that Deneuve played in her only other film for Truffaut, *Mississippi Mermaid* (1969). (I have already called attention to the evocations of the Deneuve of Buñuel's *Belle de Jour*.) (2) Depardieu's family name is "Granger." His first feature film was Marguerite Duras's *Nathalie Granger* (1971). (3) Marcel Berbert, who served as producer for so many of Truffaut's earlier movies, plays the business manager of the Théâtre Montmartre. (4) Many viewers will recognize Paulette Dubost, who plays Deneuve's faithful dresser Germaine, as the actress who played the faithful maid—faithful, that is, to her mistress, if not to her husband—in Renoir's *Rules of the Game*; these viewers will see some connection between Renoir's manic yet magisterially orchestrated threnody to the doomed Europe of 1939 and Truffaut's far more somberly ordered memorial to those dark years of occupation that followed the collapse of Renoir's Europe; those same viewers will read in the contrast between the face of Dubost in 1939 and the face of Dubost in 1980 other narratives, more specifically narratives of survival—Dubost's, France's, Renoir's (in the work of his disciple Truffaut). And as if to underscore both the timelessness of the filmed image and the flight of time that all film is fated to record, Truffaut casts as the calculating "ingenue" Nadine young Sabine Haudepin, an actress who bears in visage and in manner a marked resemblance to the young Dubost of 1939.

But one must avoid bringing these remarks to their conclusion on the suggestion that *The Last Metro* is *only* an extended excursion into cinematic reference. What had always been remarkable about Truffaut—remarkable even among his equally movie-crazed New Wave colleagues—was his capacity to attune his irresistible instinct for cinematic allusion to his utter, sometimes almost painful seriousness about the human validity of the subjects he chose for his films. This capacity was cognate with his ability—indeed, one feels, his need—to balance all the most antithetical yet rigorously exigent claims of his own temperament: the claims of sophistication and of susceptibility, of the film critic's erudition and the filmgoer's credence, of his own acute compassion and his own equally acute sense of the absurd. Who then but Truffaut could so tactfully have integrated the two principal myths implicit in the story of a man who must for years hide from the Nazis in the cellar of a theater—the myth of Anne Frank and the myth of the Phantom of the Opera?

François Truffaut

A Biographical Sketch

Mirella Jona Affron

Twenty-five years and twenty films separate François Truffaut's first feature, *The 400 Blows* (1959), from his last, *Confidentially Yours* (1983), released just one year before his death. But the preoccupation with cinema that characterized his debut—following a totally absorbing fifteen-year apprenticeship as spectator and critic—remains evident in his final work. Truffaut's obsession with his craft (and its past) is the constant element of a body of films rich in stylistic variety.

Truffaut was born in Paris in 1932. His early years were marked by the indifference of his parents and by the Second World War. Only the movie house and the enveloping fiction of film provided a refuge from home and the German occupation. By the age of fifteen, the cinema, which he had first experienced as a haven, had become an obsession to which he devoted his first sustained effort, the founding of a film club. Its almost immediate failure was of little consequence by comparison with the meeting it occasioned: that of the young Truffaut with André Bazin, already an influential film critic, soon to become (and to remain until his death in 1958) Truffaut's friend, teacher, and adviser.

Through a number of difficult years (which included stints in reform school and military prison), Bazin's protection was crucial. Crucial too was his insistence that Truffaut begin to write about film, and his assistance in publishing those writings—particularly in the landmark journal that Bazin founded with Jacques Doniol-Valcroze in 1951, *Cahiers du cinéma*. From 1953 to 1958, Truffaut wrote regularly for a number of publications (he had a weekly column in

Arts for a time), often scathingly on classic French cinema and its practitioners. Together with other young critics of the *Cahiers du cinéma* who were to become filmmakers of the New Wave—Godard, Chabrol, Rivette, Rohmer—Truffaut championed Renoir, Rossellini, Bresson, Hitchcock, and the *politique des auteurs*. The camera, he repeated after Alexandre Astruc (whose article on the *caméra-stylo*, published in 1948, is often cited as a precursor of early *Cahiers du cinéma* criticism), can be as personal an instrument as the pen or the brush. It must be wielded with the same independence and flexibility. The author of a film is the director. It is the director's vision that controls the subject, the script, the actors, the editing—the entire production. The signature of a true *auteur* is always visible, however collective the enterprise of filmmaking and whatever the constraints of the production. The making of a film need not take excessively long nor be excessively costly. And finally, the credentials of a director need not include long years of training in the studio; far more important than experience and funding are talent and invention. For Truffaut and his colleagues, the French film industry, dominated by big budgets, highly polished and anonymous studio productions (favorite targets were the direction of Claude Autant-Lara and the scripts of Jean Aurenche and Pierre Bost), was moribund.

That Truffaut should turn to directing was the logical consequence of his critical position. His first effort was a 16mm short for which friends served as crew and cast. It was followed by *Les Mistons*, a 35mm short on childhood that anticipated the subject and spirit of Truffaut's first feature film, *The 400 Blows*. Released in 1959, *The 400 Blows* followed by just one year the film that inaugurated the brightest phase of the New Wave movement (1958–1963), Claude Chabrol's *Le Beau Serge*. Nineteen fifty-nine, a truly remarkable year for the *Cahiers* group, saw also the appearance of Jean-Luc Godard's first feature film, *Breathless*, and of Chabrol's second film, *Les Cousins*. Rivette's *Paris Belongs to Us (Paris nous appartient)* appeared in 1960. But it was *The 400 Blows* that captured the award for Best Director at the Cannes Film Festival of 1959. With it, Truffaut won almost immediate international recognition.

The *400 Blows* opens a cycle of five highly personal, even autobiographical, films made between 1959 and 1978. The recurring hero, Antoine Doinel, is played by Jean-Pierre Léaud. Hero and star are contemporaries; they age together. We follow them through their maturation from adolescence to adulthood. *The 400 Blows* catches Doinel at a critical moment of his very difficult coming of age. We meet him again, at eighteen and at twenty, first as he sets out awkwardly on his own *(Antoine and Colette,* 1962), and then during a series of apprenticeships—at work and in love *(Stolen Kisses,* 1968). In his early twenties, Antoine marries and has a son *(Bed and Board,* 1970); at thirty *(Love on the Run,* 1978), Antoine is divorced and in search of love once more. In a series of flashbacks borrowed from scenes of the preceding films, *Love on the Run* illuminates Antoine's present through his past. It evokes thereby the entire cycle, synthesizing and defining Truffaut's unique rendering of the *Bildungsroman*, the novel of education, onto film, and charting the course of the first twenty years of the director's career.

During the sixties, interspersed between the first four of the Antoine Doinel series, Truffaut made seven films whose variety reflects the director's great breadth. *Shoot the Piano Player* (1960), his second feature, is partly a homage to the American gangster film, partly an experiment in the mixing of genres. *Jules and Jim* (1961) is an eccentric love story—as well as an analysis of love and friendship—set against the background of World War I and its aftermath. *Soft Skin* (1964) explores adultery in a realistically told, contemporary tale. *Fahrenheit 451* (1966), based on a Ray Bradbury science-fiction novel about book burning in the future, is Truffaut's first color film, his first film shot in a studio, and his first explicitly political subject. *The Bride Wore Black* (1967) is an exercise in the thriller mode, made just after the publication of Truffaut's long interview with

Alfred Hitchcock, and strongly imitative of the style of the master of the genre. Far more eclectic, *Mississippi Mermaid* (1969) (which, like *The Last Metro*, stars Catherine Deneuve) is a pastiche filled with references to the directors and writers Truffaut most admired. Its final shot, for example, is a direct reference to Jean Renoir's *Grand Illusion. The Wild Child* (1969) is the last film Truffaut made before completing the fourth episode of the Antoine Doinel cycle and closing the 1960s. It is the first in which, again on the model of Renoir, he assigned himself a part as actor. *The Wild Child* documents—and in a style in which we indeed recognize elements of what we think of as the "documentary"—an early nineteenth-century experiment to "civilize" a wild adolescent boy who had been found in the forest. Truffaut, clearly associated with the father figure, plays the role of narrator and tutor.

The decade of the 1970s began with *The Two English Girls* (1971), the story of an unconventional triangle reminiscent both of *Jules and Jim* (which, like *The Two English Girls*, was based on a novel by Henri-Pierre Roché) and of the Doinel cycle (Jean-Pierre Léaud plays the lead role). *Such a Gorgeous Kid Like Me* (1972) was finished hurriedly the next year. Truffaut was eager to begin work on *Day for Night* (1973), the film he had long waited to make about the making of a film. It is often considered, with *The 400 Blows* and *Jules and Jim*, one of Truffaut's most inspired works. His passion for the conventions of the medium (expressed in the variety of exercises in genre that dominated the films of the 1960s), his admiration for the craft of the American studio film (to which homage is paid in the French title, *La Nuit américaine*), and above all his devotion to the society of actors and technicians, are reflected in the double role he plays: behind the camera as director of *Day for Night* and before the camera as director of the film within the film.

The success of *Day for Night* was followed by that of *The Story of Adele H.* (1975), whose script was adapted from the nineteenth-century diaries of one of the daughters of Victor Hugo. The remarkable depiction of the love-crazed heroine that Truffaut elicits from Isabelle Adjani (a number of scenes of *Day for Night* give a sense of the intelligence and attention Truffaut expended upon the direction of actors) can be added to the list of memorable performances that includes those of Léaud (*The 400 Blows*), Charles Aznavour (*Shoot the Piano Player*), Jeanne Moreau (*Jules and Jim*), Valentina Cortese (*Day for Night*), and Catherine Deneuve (*The Last Metro*).

Four films make up the production of the 1970s: *Small Change* (1976) is a return to the theme of childhood; *The Man Who Loved Women* (1977) and

The Green Room (1978) are treatments of obsessional behavior, the latter starring Truffaut once more and based largely on Henry James's short story "Altar of the Dead"; the last is *Love on the Run*.

The decade of the 1980s opened with the making of *The Last Metro*, a film about the theater, part two of Truffaut's projected trilogy on performance. (The treatment of the cinema, *Day for Night*, constitutes part one; a film on the music hall, Truffaut's third passion, was to complete the series.) *The Woman Next Door* (1981) starred Gérard Depardieu (who appeared in *The Last Metro* with Catherine Deneuve) and launched the film career of Fanny Ardant. Her performance in *Confidentially Yours* (1983) embodies the style of the American romantic thriller, and returned the director one last time to an explicit expression of his preoccupation with film and its traditions.

The Last Metro

The Last Metro

hat follows is the transcription of the verbal and visual continuity of the release print of *The Last Metro*. According to Truffaut, no finished shooting script was used in the production of the film. Our work was checked against the text of *Le Dernier Métro* that appeared in the French periodical *L'Avant-Scène Cinéma*, nos. 303–4 (1–15 March 1983). The French text was established by Dominique Haas and introduced by Truffaut.

The abbreviations used to describe camera distance follow the usual English-language conventions: (e.g., ELS=extreme long shot, MS=medium shot, MCU=medium close-up, etc.). We urge the reader to remember that these terms are at best approximative. Descriptions of camera movement have been phrased in the least technical terms possible. Because of restrictions of space, full verbal analysis of camera placement and movement has been limited to those shots requiring such information to clarify the image for the reader.

Also because of space restrictions, we have had to suppress many details that contribute to the viewer's experience of the actual film. For example, there is no reference to music played outside the film's spaces and unheard by the characters; there is very limited reference to costume and to such details of background as shop windows, posters, and so forth, or to the entrances and exits of characters who do not contribute significantly to the main narrative action of the shot. Similarly, many passing phrases (e.g., "hellos" or "good-byes" in group scenes) have not always been recorded here. And novelistic notations, especially those arising from our interpretation of the characters' motivations, have been kept to a minimum.

Shots have been numbered for easy cross-reference.

Although we worked together closely on all aspects of this edition, the verbal continuity and translation are mainly the work of Mirella Jona Affron, the visual continuity the work of E. Rubinstein.

Credits and Cast

Over the credits, we hear "Mon Amant de Saint-Jean" ("My Lover of Saint-Jean"). The words run as follows: "I don't know why I went dancing / On the holiday of Saint-Jean, in the dance hall; / It took but a single kiss / To make a prisoner of my heart. // How can you not lose your head / When bold arms hold you close? / You always believe in love's sweet words / When they're spoken by the eyes. // To me, who loved him so much / He seemed the handsomest man of Saint-Jean; / He left me tipsy, without any willpower / Beneath his kisses. // Without tears or hesitation, I gave him / The best part of my being; / That fast talker, every time he lied to me / I knew it—but I loved him. // How can you not lose your head. . . ."

Direction
François Truffaut

Story
François Truffaut, Suzanne Schiffman

Screenplay
François Truffaut, Suzanne Schiffman, Jean-Claude Grumberg

Cinematography
Nestor Almendros, assisted by Florent Bazin, Emilio Paccul-Latorre, Tessa Racine

Art Direction
Jean-Pierre Kohut-Svelko, assisted by Pierre Gompertz, Jacques Leguillon, Roland Jacob

Properties
Jacques Preisach

Sound
Michel Laurent, assisted by Michel Mellier

Sound Effects
Daniel Couteau

Mixing
Jacques Maumont

Assistant Director
Suzanne Schiff.nan, assisted by Emmanuel Clot, Alain Tasma

Script Continuity
Christine Pellé

Costumes
Lisele Roos, assisted by Christiane Aumar-Fageol, Edwige Cherel, Françoise Poillot

Make-Up
Didier Lavergne, Thi Loan N'Guyen,
Françoise Ben Soussan

Hair Styles
Jean-Pierre Berroyer, Nadine Leroy

Stage Manager
Jean-Louis Godfroy

Still Photographs
Jean-Pierre Fizet

Production Administrator
Henry Dutrannoy

Electricians
Jean-Pierre Gasché, André Seybald,
Serge Valézy

Gaffers
Charles Freess, Jacques Fréjabue,
Gérard Bougeant

Music
Georges Delerue

Editing
Martine Barraqué, Marie-Aimée
Debril, Jean-François Giré

Production Manager
Jean-José Richer, assisted by Roland
Thénot

A production of Les Films du
Carrosse, Sedif s.a.—t.f.1—Société
Française de Production

Excerpts from *La Disparue* (*The
Vanished One*), a play by Karen
Bergen, translated from the
Norwegian by Aïna Bellis

Songs
"Bei Mir Bist du Schön"—music by
Sholom Secunda, words by Cahn-
Chaplin, Jacob Jacobs, Jacques
Larue (Editions Chappell)
"Prière à Zumba"—by A. Lara,
Jacques Larue (Editions F. Day-
Disque Pathé-Marconi)
"Mon Amant de Saint-Jean"—by
E. Carrara, L. Agel (Edition
Méridian-Disque Pathé-Marconi.
EMI C 178 15404/5); sung by
Lucienne Delyle
"Sombréros et Mantilles—by J.
Vaissade-Chanty (Edition Méridian-
Disque Pathé-Marconi. EMI C 178
15416/17); sung by Rina Ketty
"Cantique: Pitié Mon Dieu"—by A.
Kunk

Length: 128 minutes

Marion Steiner
Catherine Deneuve

Bernard Granger
Gérard Depardieu

Jean-Loup Cottins
Jean Poiret

Lucas Steiner
Heinz Bennent

Arlette Guillaume
Andréa Ferréol

Germaine Fabre
Paulette Dubost

Nadine Marsac
Sabine Haudepin

Daxiat
Jean-Louis Richard

Raymond, the Stage Manager
Maurice Risch

Merlin
Marcel Berbert

Gestapo Agent
Richard Bohringer

Christian Léglise
Jean-Pierre Klein

Jacquot
Master Franck Pasquier

German Nightclub Singer
Rénata

René Bernardini
Jean-José Richer

Martine
Martine Simonet

Lieutenant Bergen
Laszlo Szabo

Yvonne, the Chambermaid
Hénia Ziv

Rosette Goldstern
Jessica Zucman

Marc
Alain Tasma

Valentin
René Dupré

Desk Clerk
Pierre Bélot

Bernard's Replacement
Christian Baltauss

First Nurse
Alexandra Aumond

Second Nurse
Marie-Dominique Henry

Rosen
Jacob Weizbluth

Boys' Choir
Les Petits Chanteurs
de l'Abbaye

Jacquot's Mother (Concierge)
Rose Thierry

The Continuity Script

*1 to 14. A montage of shots depicting German-occupied Paris, as follows:
1. ELS of a Paris street, dominated by a Nazi flag; camera zooms in to the
swastika in the center of the flag. 2. ELS of the facade of a building; camera
tilts down from the words "Chamber of Deputies" on the lintel to a traffic
signpost bearing many indicators, all in German.* [1] *3. A map of France
superimposed on a photograph of a sea of faces. The northern sector, in black,
is marked by a swastika and the site of Paris; the southern sector, in yellow, by
a dot locating Vichy. 4. Freeze ELS of Parisians on a street. 5. Freeze MS of
two Nazi officers and a French woman talking on a street. 6. ELS of a metro
station, figures rushing from the foreground toward trains. 7. MS of the
interior of a butcher shop, various cuts of meat hanging from racks. 8. MCS
of faces of Parisians looking into the shop. 9 to 13. Various shots of billboards
advertising* La Symphonie fantastique, *Emil Jannings in* Le Président Krüger,
and Olga Tschechowa and Ilse Werner in Bel Ami; [2] *13 closes with an* ECU
*examination of seductive, slanted female eyes painted on the billboard.
14. "Théâtre Montmartre"* [3] *is spelled out in flashing marquee bulbs; the
background emerges as a photograph of Lucas Steiner's face. Camera moves
in; the flashing words disappear and shot ends in* ECU *of Lucas Steiner's eyes.
Fade to black.*

During this montage, the following off-screen narration is heard:

VOICE-OVER: Paris, September, 1942. For two years, the German army has
occupied the northern part of France. The separation between the Occupied
Zone and the Free Zone constitutes a kind of border that cuts horizontally
across the country. In the Occupied Zone, curfew empties out the streets
after eleven o'clock in the evening, and for Parisians it is terribly important
not to miss the last metro. Because they are hungry, Parisians wait in line for
hours to buy a little food; because their homes are cold they crowd each
evening into theaters. Cinemas and legitimate theaters play to full houses;
seats must be reserved well in advance. At the Théâtre Montmartre a play is
in rehearsal, and yet the director, Lucas Steiner, has had to leave France in a
great rush. He had no choice.

15. The street alongside the Théâtre Montmartre. The action begins as Arlette enters at left, pursued by Bernard. Camera follows their progress, always to the right, in MS *range. At certain points, Arlette turns to face her pursuer; at other points, Bernard pushes ahead of Arlette to block her progress.*

BERNARD: Excuse me, Mademoiselle, excuse me. I saw you and I'd like—

ARLETTE: You want the time? It's twenty minutes to seven.

BERNARD (*looking at his wrist*): No, thank you, I know that. I have a watch.

ARLETTE: Then you must be lost. Perhaps you're trying to find your way.

BERNARD (*gesturing to left*): No, no, no, not at all. This is my neighborhood.

ARLETTE: Good-bye, then.

BERNARD: No, no, wait. I wouldn't want you to think that I'm trying to pick you up. (*Arlette laughs.*) But no, it's true.

ARLETTE: What would make me think such a thing?

BERNARD: I was in a café. I was making a phone call, I saw you, and I don't know, your eyes, your expression . . . I said to myself—

ARLETTE: You said to yourself?

BERNARD: Today is my lucky day. I found myself all alone and I thought that we could have a drink and talk . . .

ARLETTE (*her amusement now clearly waning*): Listen, I'm not thirsty and I have nothing to say. Let me get by.

BERNARD: You're obviously mistaken about me. You think that I do this every day. No . . .

ARLETTE (*facing him and smiling ironically*): Only every other day. You're starting to bore me.

BERNARD: O.K. Have it your way. Look, there's no reason why I shouldn't explain myself. Please. Do you know what it is to feel attracted? You've got to believe me. I haven't approached a woman I didn't know for four years.

ARLETTE: So I should feel particularly honored? Listen, I've had enough. Do you want a public scene?

BERNARD: Think it over. I want *something*. A name, an address. Do you have a telephone? My name is Bernard.

ARLETTE: You want my phone number? You simply have to have it?

BERNARD (*removing a notebook*): Oh, yes. Terrific. I'll write it down.

ARLETTE: ODEON 84-00.

16. BERNARD (MCU, *writing on what seems to be the script of a play*): That's ODEON 84-00. ODEON 84-00. You're putting me on. That's the number for the right time!

17. LS *of Arlette walking toward, then out of, frame right, looking over her shoulder at Bernard and laughing.*

18. Resume on Bernard, as in 16. Dismayed, he turns toward frame left, where he soon moves to exit.

19. The square in front of the Théâtre Montmartre. Shot begins with a small boy entering frame at left foreground. He proceeds rightward, eventually into LS *range, playfully marching with his left foot on the curb and his right foot in the road.*

FEMALE VOICE (*off-screen*): Who is that kid?
SECOND FEMALE VOICE (*off-screen*): That's Jacquot, the son of the
   concierge. Yes, the concierge of the theater.

Jacquot arrives at a pile of sandbags, which he proceeds to kick. Entering frame right, a German soldier passes him and affectionately pats his head, then passes out of frame left; Jacquot's mother, hastening in the opposite direction, passes the soldier. She grabs Jacquot's arm and leads him toward camera.

JACQUOT'S MOTHER: What did that guy do to you?
JACQUOT: He didn't do anything to me. He touched my hair.
JACQUOT'S MOTHER: O.K., let's go home. We're going to wash your hair.
   Quick.

Jacquot breaks away from her and runs to the right, away from camera; she pursues him and grabs his arm.

JACQUOT'S MOTHER: Jacques, come here. That's enough now. Let's go.

Firmly in hand, Jacquot is led leftward as camera follows; as Jacquot and his mother pass out of frame left, Bernard, hands in pocket, crosses their path from the same point. Moving toward camera, he steps off the curb into the road; camera follows his walk to a doorway marked "Théâtre Montmartre"; Bernard knocks and waits, looks about, walks again toward camera, then left, out of frame; as he exits, two little girls playing hopscotch, entering from frame left, cross his path and move to center frame.

20. The narrow street alongside the theater. As several people are seen going about their business, Bernard walks toward camera. As he enters MS *range, and as a recording of a woman singing is heard on the soundtrack, Bernard turns toward a door labeled "Concierge." When no one comes to the door, he moves back left toward the window in the same flat and reaches forward to knock.*

21. The concierge's window. The window is open, revealing Jacquot's Mother washing Jacquot's hair.

JACQUOT'S MOTHER: What is it?
BERNARD: Hello. Is the theater closed? Actually, I have an appointment.
JACQUOT'S MOTHER: Have you tried the stage door, over there, behind you?

22. The window, Bernard outside and Jacquot's Mother within.

BERNARD: Thanks.

He starts to close the window.

JACQUOT'S MOTHER: Just leave it.

Camera follows as Bernard turns and crosses the alley to the stage door. He climbs the outside stairs and addresses Raymond, who stands in the doorway.

BERNARD: Hello. I think I have an appointment.
RAYMOND: Oh, so you're Bernard Granger.
BERNARD: Yes.
RAYMOND: Right, of course. You're expected. I'll take you up to Madame Steiner.

Bernard enters the stage door and disappears into the hallway that leads backstage.

23. Camera follows Bernard and Raymond as they pass from the backstage and across the stage itself on their way to the corridors of the backstage area.

BERNARD (*alone on the stage and facing the empty auditorium*): Nice theater.
RAYMOND (*off-screen*): A bit different from the Grand Guignol.[4]
BERNARD (*staring into the empty theater*): Twice as large, at least. I've been here before, but in the audience. I saw Madame Steiner in Chekhov's *Cherry Orchard*. (*Turns to Raymond, who has reentered from the right.*) Is there any news of Lucas Steiner?
RAYMOND: The boss? He had a close call. One day they came looking for him here.
BERNARD: Here? In the theater? Germans?
RAYMOND: No, French. They were everywhere. They had the building surrounded. That same morning Lucas Steiner had beat it out of Paris.
BERNARD: I was told he went to America.
RAYMOND: Yes, South America. Some place over there.

24. Raymond and Bernard emerge from the doorway onto a landing.

RAYMOND: I hope he's able to find work. (*The two move down a short corridor.*) This is the way to the manager's office.
MERLIN (*entering the corridor from frame right*): Good evening, Raymond.
RAYMOND: Good evening, Monsieur Merlin. Bernard Granger, Monsieur Merlin.

MERLIN (*shaking Bernard's hand*): Yes, I recognize you. Good evening.
BERNARD: Good evening. Happy to meet you.

25. RAYMOND (*leading Bernard up the stairs to the second floor*): Monsieur Merlin is our business manager. In money matters, you'll deal with him.

Raymond and Bernard arrive at the second floor. Frame is dominated by an open door. To the right of the door sits a small, melancholy man.

RAYMOND (*pointing to the doorway*): Wait here for a minute.
BERNARD (*coming through the doorway*): Thank you.
RAYMOND (*closing the door, which is marked "Administration" [i.e., "Management"]*): Madame Steiner will be here in a minute.
BERNARD: O.K.

Camera holds briefly on the closed door and the man waiting outside.

26. MS *of Bernard in the office. He is drawn to a seating-plan design of the theater, which he touches, then to a large model of the Eiffel Tower. He notices and picks up a photograph of Marion Steiner in black fin de siècle winter costume* (The Cherry Orchard?). *As he hears the door opening, he turns to face frame left.*

27 to 32. *Intercut with* MC *reaction shots of Bernard, intently watching and listening, are shots (from Bernard's point of view) of Marion and Jean-Loup Cottins arguing in the adjoining room. As Marion and Jean-Loup talk, they pass (always in* LS *range) from an open doorway at the right to an open doorway at the left and back again; camera tracks the wall (covered with theatrical photos, etc.) that separates the doorways when Marion and Jean-Loup temporarily pass out of view behind it.*

JEAN-LOUP: Listen, Marion, I know as well as you that Rosen's Aryan Certificate is forged. But, believe me, no one will check it under a magnifying glass.
MARION: He doesn't even have a work permit.
JEAN-LOUP: He'll claim that he lost his card and so he'll be able to get a duplicate. With our contacts, we should be able—
MARION: We'll have to save our contacts for more important things.

JEAN-LOUP: But Marion, with these papers Rosen is still able to work. He says that on the set of *Père Goriot* at the Billancourt studios, no one bothers him about it.[5]

MARION: If they are so careless at the Billancourt, so much the better for him. But here we follow the regulations to the letter. No work permit, no job.

JEAN-LOUP (*opening a doorway to the corridor*): What am I going to say to Rosen?

MARION: All you have to do is tell the truth: Marion Steiner doesn't want Jews in her theater.

JEAN-LOUP (*off-screen*): Rosen, if you'll follow me.

33. In MS *range, the "Administration" door is opened and Rosen and Jean-Loup enter; Bernard is in the right foreground.*

JEAN-LOUP (*to Bernard*): No one told me you were here. Give me two seconds, please.

BERNARD: O.K.

Jean-Loup reroutes Rosen back through the "Administration" door.

JEAN-LOUP (*to Bernard*): I'll be right back. I'm going to find Marion.

Alone before the closed door, Bernard hears:

ROSEN (*off-screen*): So, Monsieur Cottins. Have you explained my case to Madame Steiner?

34. MLS *of Marion, pacing in the space framed by the left doorway.*

ROSEN (*off-screen*): What did she say?

35. Resume MCU *of Bernard.*

JEAN-LOUP (*off-screen*): Look, Rosen, I'm terribly sorry, but she doesn't want Jewish actors in her theater.

36. MS *of the translucent pane of the "Administration" door, through which Jean-Loup and Rosen are seen in silhouette.*

ROSEN: Now I've heard everything. I would have expected that answer from anyone else. But to hear this in Lucas Steiner's own theater, that's really the limit.

Rosen puts on his hat and exits in silhouette past Jean-Loup.

37. MCS of Bernard moving toward the "Administration" door. As he opens the door and exits, Jean-Loup is approaching him. They stand framed in MS in the doorway.

JEAN-LOUP: Come in.
BERNARD: Wait, wait. I want to understand.
JEAN-LOUP: What?
BERNARD: Look. I was very happy to have a chance to act in a real theater, in a real play. But if I have to lower my pants to prove that I'm not Jewish, well then, no thank you.
JEAN-LOUP (*imploringly*): No, no, no.
BERNARD: No, thank you. And furthermore, I am not interested in taking someone else's role.
JEAN-LOUP: No, no, no. There's a misunderstanding. The actor I was obliged to turn down was not being considered for the role of the tutor. He was to play the gamekeeper who has a tiny scene at the end of the third act.
BERNARD: Because . . .
JEAN-LOUP: No, no, believe me.
BERNARD: Under these conditions I really . . .
JEAN-LOUP: Believe me, Granger, I wanted you from the very beginning for Marion's leading man. You have to understand. We're not even sure we'll be allowed to perform. The text of the play is still with the censor, and we haven't yet had an answer.

Marion enters the doorway frame at the left.

JEAN-LOUP: Ah, Marion, I want to introduce you to Bernard Granger.
MARION: Hello.
BERNARD: How do you do.

Camera follows Marion as she walks through the doorway into the office, seating herself behind the desk.

MARION: I've heard wonderful things about you. I spoke with some people who went to the Grand Guignol for the first time expressly to see you perform. (*By now, Bernard is standing at the left of the desk.*) And then, Jean-Loup is seldom wrong.

38. BERNARD (*in* MCS): When they asked me to play at the Grand Guignol I wasn't sure whether I should take the part, but I really got a kick out of *The Skeleton in the Closet.*

39 to 45. Alternating shots of Bernard at left of desk and Marion seated behind it. Shots begin in MC *range but then move into* CU. *Marion's beauty and elegance, and Bernard's intense interest in her, become plain.*

MARION: Unfortunately I couldn't come see you perform because I don't get out in the evening. My husband used to look after everything and I took a certain pleasure in understanding nothing of the paperwork, regulations, financial matters. (*She is busily signing various documents.*) I've had to learn very quickly. We need to talk about your contract.
BERNARD: What? Here? Now?
MARION: Yes. Here. Now. It will be all done. Tell me, how much did they pay you at the Grand Guignol?

46. Shot begins with Jean-Loup walking away from camera down a long corridor. As he nears the end of the corridor, Nadine enters from a doorway at the left.

JEAN-LOUP: I was just looking for you. Here's the script. It makes edifying reading. Meditate on it, my child.

Jean-Loup and Nadine walk toward camera. Germaine, carrying a dress on a hanger, enters the corridor behind them from a doorway at the right.

GERMAINE (*pointing to the dress*): Is this the one?
NADINE (*looking back at Germaine*): Yes, yes, thank you.

Germaine disappears into the doorway at the left from which Nadine had emerged.

NADINE (*to Jean-Loup*): I'm glad. Because I went to the drama bookshop yesterday and they didn't have a copy.
JEAN-LOUP: It's not published.

By now, Jean-Loup and Nadine have entered MS *range and turned left.*

NADINE: I've never heard of this play.
JEAN-LOUP: It's a Norwegian play, written by a Norwegian woman playwright, Karen Bergen. How Norwegian can you get! Lucas unearthed it. It's translated from the Norwegian. You don't know any Norwegian?
NADINE: Hardly!
JEAN-LOUP: Neither do I. I promise you that the critics won't hesitate to pan the translation just the same.

Marion enters from the right, then crosses left.

MARION (*shaking hands*): Hello, Nadine.
NADINE: Hello, Marion.
MARION (*extending her hand to Jean-Loup, who gives her a copy of the play, then to Nadine*): Do you know Bernard Granger?
NADINE: Why? Is he here?
MARION: Yes, he's in my office.
NADINE: Oh. No, I don't know him. (*Camera follows Nadine as she crosses right to the office door.*) But we once nearly met. (*Nadine looks through the office door at Bernard, who is seated at the desk, signing a contract.*) Hi. We once nearly met at a mutual friend's, at Lucien's. You were supposed to come to his housewarming party.
BERNARD: Ah, Moussalier, yes, I couldn't make it. But we'll get to know each other. I'm signing a contract.

47 to 49. Two CUs *of a document awaiting Bernard's signature, interrupted by a* CU *of Bernard's face as he reads it.*

BERNARD: I hereby declare that I am not Jewish, and that to the best of my knowledge none of my parents or my grandparents are or were Jewish.

Under the date—8 October 1942—Bernard signs.

50. Bernard and Raymond cross paths on the landing off the stage.

RAYMOND: Everything all right?
BERNARD: It's all settled.
RAYMOND: Good. Now we'll get to see a lot of each other.
BERNARD: Very good.
RAYMOND: So long.
BERNARD: So long.

51. Marion and Jean-Loup descend the stairs from the second floor, moving toward camera.

JEAN-LOUP: You never really wanted to be an actress.
MARION: I had a profession that I liked.
JEAN-LOUP: If Lucas hadn't pulled you out of your high-fashion house you'd still be draped in expensive rags. Own up.
MARION (*cheerfully*): Quite right. And you don't know the whole story. If I had refused to go off with him, he would have asked Mademoiselle Chanel to fire me. He told me so himself.
JEAN-LOUP: That sounds just like him.

The conversation has taken Marion and Jean-Loup past Raymond's booth.

RAYMOND (*emerging*): Shall I turn off the master switch, Madame Steiner?
MARION: Yes.

Raymond retreats into the booth and pulls the switch, plunging most of the house into darkness. He leaves the booth, closing the door behind him.

52. Marion and Jean-Loup move toward the stage door, where Marc is waiting.

JEAN-LOUP (*to Marc*): You're here.
MARC: I was waiting for you, Jean-Loup.
JEAN-LOUP: Yes, yes, that's right. (*He looks outside the door.*) Damn, it's Daxiat.[6] I have a date with him for dinner. You're on your own. I'll see you later.
MARC: O.K. Good night.

JEAN-LOUP: Good night. (*Crosses back to Marion.*) Stay back here. Marion, I forgot to tell you . . .

MARION: Tell me what?

JEAN-LOUP: Daxiat. I agreed to have dinner with him. Look, after all, he can help us with the censor's permit. I even hinted that you might join us.

MARION: Well, you shouldn't have. And I don't understand how you can spend an evening with that man.

JEAN-LOUP: One doesn't always have a choice.

MARION: You know the excuse he used for banning *Britannicus*.[7]

JEAN-LOUP: Yes, I know. I know. He said it was an effeminate production. I know, I know.

Jean-Loup again goes to the door and peers out. Now, through the doorway, we see Daxiat in the alleyway. Camera holds on Daxiat as Jean-Loup retreats out of view at frame right.

JEAN-LOUP (*off-screen*): But we need him for the permit, don't we? So I'm asking you to say hello, and to shake his hand as well.

MARION (*off-screen*): I'll say hello and I'll shake his hand. As for dinner, make up an excuse. I'm tired. I'm going back to the hotel.

Marion and Jean-Loup reenter frame and pass through the door.

MARION: Raymond, you can turn everything off.

Camera pans to Raymond, who pulls a switch to extinguish the remaining lights, then takes his bicycle from its hook on the wall.

53. Marion and Jean-Loup move away from camera into the alley, where they greet Daxiat, who stands near his expensive black car. Daxiat and Marion shake hands.

54. MS of Raymond, watching.

55. Resume, somewhat closer, on the alley. Jean-Loup first kisses Marion, who departs; then he enters Daxiat's car, which drives out of frame. In the background, the café's curtains are drawn for the night.

56. Orchestra floor of the theater. Marc stands at the director's table, watching the stage. He turns on a lamp. The play is in rehearsal.

MARION (*off-screen*): "That's fine, Eric, you can go to bed now."
JEAN-LOUP (*off-screen*): Eric hesitates for a moment . . .

57. On stage. Bernard, Jean-Loup, Marion, and Nadine are arranged in a semicircle, all seated except Jean-Loup, as they read through the play.

JEAN-LOUP (*continuing*): . . . before leaving the room. Then he turns toward his mother: "Mother, is Monsieur Carl going to come?"
MARION: "I don't know, my child. What do you think?"
JEAN-LOUP: "Yes, I think so. I think he will come back."

58. MS of Raymond, painting a stool and watching the stage.

59. Resume on stage group.

JEAN-LOUP: Helena, startled by the noise, drops the emboidery hoop she was holding in her hands. Carl draws back and—
BERNARD: "Is someone there?"
JEAN-LOUP: —he sees Helena.
BERNARD: "Why are you hiding?"
MARION: "I didn't want to see you. Leave this house. Your presence here is harmful."
BERNARD: "Fine. I think I will leave. But first hear me out. When Doctor Sanders hired me last spring, I was told . . ."

During the last moments of this read-through, Jean-Loup, Nadine, and Marion have all acknowledged the arrival of someone out of frame, left: first Nadine, then Marion leave frame to greet her.

JEAN-LOUP (*to Bernard*): Let's see if it's better the other way around: "Last spring, when . . ."

Now Jean-Loup also moves to greet the new arrival, who, we see, is Arlette.

60. MS *of Bernard, who continues to work on his lines by himself. Now Jean-Loup, too, has left the rehearsal to greet the newcomer. Bernard's reading of his lines and Jean-Loup's greetings to Arlette merge on the soundtrack.*

JEAN-LOUP (*walking back toward Bernard and touching his shoulder*): I'd like to introduce you.
BERNARD (*rising*): Ah, yes.

He and Jean-Loup move toward Arlette.

JEAN-LOUP: Our designer, Arlette Guillaume, who will do the sets and the costumes. My dear, I'd like to introduce Bernard Granger, who will play Carl.
ARLETTE: Hello.
JEAN-LOUP (*off-screen*): You've certainly seen him on the stage.
ARLETTE: No, I don't think so.

61. CU *of Arlette, over Bernard's shoulder. Her expression has changed with her recognition of him.*

ARLETTE: Yes, yes of course, I've seen him before.
JEAN-LOUP (*off-screen*): At the Grand Guignol, of course.
ARLETTE: No, it was in a much more ordinary role. He was playing a man cruising the streets.

62. BERNARD (CU *over Arlette's shoulder*): You mustn't judge me by that role. I was improvising a part.

63. ARLETTE (*as in 61*): And yet I would have sworn that you knew it by heart.

64. JEAN-LOUP (MCS): O.K., my friends, the rehearsal is over. (*He moves right.*) But I'd like to say something.

65. Resume on Raymond, watching the stage.

JEAN-LOUP (*off-screen*): I will be staging *The Vanished One.*

66. Resume on Jean-Loup as in 64, but now he moves left, toward Marion and the others.

JEAN-LOUP: There is no need to tell you that, like the rest of you, I would very much have preferred that Lucas be the director . . . Fortunately, it so happens that before departing he left some notes . . .

67 to 71. Montage of shots of Jean-Loup as he continues his speech and of various characters listening.

JEAN-LOUP: . . . some extensive notes, on the manner in which he expected to stage the play. Obviously, I will be guided as much as possible by these notes. And of course I will be completely available to help you. That's it.

72. Arlette, Marion, Nadine, and Jean-Loup on stage.

NADINE: If you don't need me any more, I'll take off.
JEAN-LOUP: Yes, run along, my dear.

They all exchange farewells; Nadine exits.

ARLETTE: The newspaperman from *Je suis partout*, your friend Daxiat . . .[8]

73. MCS of Bernard.

ARLETTE (*off-screen*): . . . couldn't he help us keep the epilepsy scene?
JEAN-LOUP (*off-screen*): He already helped us get the censor's permit.

Meanwhile, Bernard has turned to follow Nadine to the door.

NADINE: Bernard, can you help me with my bracelet? The clasp is stuck on account of the chain. (*Bernard takes her hand.*) Do you read palms?
BERNARD: Of course.

74 to 76. Shots of Bernard reading Nadine's palm intercut with CUS of Marion observing them from the stage.

NADINE: Go on then. What do you see?
BERNARD: I see that there are two women in you.
NADINE: That's for sure.

77. The staircase to the second floor.

GERMAINE (*climbing into view and then out of frame*): Raymond, come
   quickly, I'm afraid. I hear some noise in the theater.

78 to 80. The empty theater.

RAYMOND (*off-screen*): Don't worry, Germaine, I'll go check. (*He enters
   frame, inspecting.*) Is someone here? Anyone here? (*He catches sight of
   someone hidden in one of the side orchestra loges.*) What are you doing in
   there, Martine? How did you get in?
MARTINE: Through the door. I saw the rehearsal. It was wonderful.
RAYMOND: But Martine, I told you to wait outside. You don't do one god-
   damn thing I tell you.
MARTINE: Calm down, please. Look at what I brought. (*Shows him a large
   object wrapped in a checkered cloth.*) Are you still interested? I had no
   money. I have to pay for it tonight, or else bring it back.
RAYMOND: How much?
MARTINE: Forty-two hundred francs.
RAYMOND: Wow.
MARTINE: But it weighs more than fifteen pounds.
RAYMOND: Madame Steiner is in the other room. I'll go see.

*81. While shot holds mainly on Marion and Bernard in MS range, the
characters associated with the production enter and leave frame, exchanging
evening farewells; only the most important interruptions are noted here.*

MARION: Let's see, the Grand Guignol has a little more than one hundred seats
   in the orchestra, sixty or so in the balcony. That means about two hundred
   when the house is full. Is half a house about average?
BERNARD: Yes, that's it. A little more on Sunday, a little less on weekdays.
   But on the average, that's it—half full.

MARION: With each seat at between twenty and forty francs, that makes six thousand francs each evening.
RAYMOND (*entering from foreground*): Madame Steiner?
MARION: Yes? Are there many of you on the stage? Excuse me.

Camera follows Marion and Raymond as they move left, outside Bernard's hearing. Raymond whispers a message; Marion replies "Yes" and returns to the original set-up with Bernard.

BERNARD: Yes. There are four of us. Three play at least two roles each.
MARION: So six thousand francs, and the cost of the set, and under half you'd lose money.

Nadine enters frame, inserting herself behind and between Marion and Bernard.

NADINE: I'm ready. Shall we go?
BERNARD: Yes.
NADINE (*to Marion*): Good night.
MARION: Good night.
BERNARD: Good night, Madame Steiner.
MARION: Good night.

Nadine and Bernard leave frame. Camera moves in on

MARION (*who says to herself*): "Good night, Madame Steiner. Good night, Marion."

She walks out of frame at right.

82 to 84. High-angle LS *of Bernard and Nadine in the alley behind the theater, in front of the café, talking and then going off together, intercut with* CS *of Marion at a window, looking down at them.*

85. MARION (in CU, *still watching through the window, hears a knock*): Come in.

86. Raymond enters the door to Marion's offices. Camera unobtrusively follows Marion and Raymond as they move freely about the rooms and the corridor outside the door.

RAYMOND: I have your ham, Madame Steiner. It's forty-two hundred.
MARION: Forty-two hundred francs?
RAYMOND: Yes, but it's over fifteen pounds. If you think it's too expensive, I can return it easily.
MARION (*moving to her desk to get the money*): No, no, I'll keep it. It will last all winter.

Raymond retreats to fetch a cello case.

MARION: Forty-two hundred, right?
RAYMOND: Yes, yes, forty-two hundred.

He places the cello case on the day bed.

MARION: Here you are.
RAYMOND: Thank you. Here's the cello.
MARION: What am I to do with a cello?
RAYMOND (*laughing, opening the case, and removing the wrapped ham*): And here's the animal. Look at it. Fifteen pounds. Fifteen. I thought of the cello case because you couldn't very well walk into the hotel with a ham under your arm. Did I do the wrong thing?
MARION: No, no. That's fine. It was a very good idea, Raymond. Thank you.
RAYMOND: I'm off, Madame Steiner. Don't forget the lights and please close the shutters. The new air-raid warden is a bastard.

He exits through the "Administration" door.

MARION (*closing the door behind Raymond*): O.K. Good night.

She walks toward the cello case on the day bed, pauses, lifts the case and hides it behind some costumes hanging on a rack, then turns out the light and exits.

87. High-angle ELS *of the Seine and a bridge; camera tracks across the quay to the facade of a building, on which the sign "Hotel du Pont Neuf" is superimposed.*

88. ELS *of the hotel lobby. The scene is dominated by German officers. Camera tracks Marion from the rear as she crosses the lobby toward the hotel desk. In* MC *range, a white-haired French gentleman greets her:*

VALENTIN: Marion.

MARION: Yes?

VALENTIN (*announcing himself*): Valentin.

MARION: Oh, Valentin. Excuse me. I am so distracted. How stupid of me.

VALENTIN: No, no, no. I beg you. Don't excuse yourself. I know I've aged a great deal. I left a manuscript with the desk clerk. A script. Take your time reading it. You'll let me know. I don't want to keep you. Good-bye.

MARION: Good-bye, Valentin.

She watches him exit, then continues toward the desk, camera still tracking her from the rear.

DESK CLERK: Good evening. This envelope is for you.

MARION (*taking the envelope*): Yes, I know.

The clerk reaches for her room key and gives it to her; she thanks him.

DESK CLERK: May I speak with you for a moment?

He moves toward frame right from behind the desk; she moves to join him as camera follows her past a Nazi officer at a house phone conducting a conversation in German. Now Marion and the Clerk stand somewhat apart, in MC *range.*

DESK CLERK: This is what I wanted to mention to you. I keep getting mail addressed to Monsieur Steiner, probably from persons who don't know that he's not at the hotel. I'm very embarrassed about this. Do you want me to return the mail to the senders saying that Monsieur Steiner is not here anymore or would you rather I gave it to you?

MARION (*looking at the letters*): I think it's probably business mail for the theater. Yes, that's it. I'll take it.

DESK CLERK: Fine. If other mail should arrive, should I give it to you in the same manner?

MARION: Yes.

DESK CLERK: Perfect.

MARION: Thank you.

She exits right.

DESK CLERK: You're welcome. Good-bye, Madame Steiner.

Exits left, back toward the desk.

89. *Marion enters the doorway of her hotel room. Yvonne, the chambermaid, is at left, at first out of frame. Camera follows Marion left as she crosses, then holds on Marion and Yvonne for a moment, then follows Yvonne right as she crosses to the door.*

MARION: Good evening, Yvonne.

YVONNE: Good evening, Madame. Will you dine in your room?

MARION: No, thank you. I ate at the theater.

YVONNE: Very well. Good night, Madame.

MARION: Good night.

YVONNE (*showing concern and pausing at the door*): Did the newspaperman from *Mirror of Paris* call you?

MARION (*off-screen*): No, why?

YVONNE: That's odd. I was here at noon to wake up your room and he was standing in the hallway with a camera.

90. *Camera picks up on Marion in MC range and follows her as she paces somewhat uneasily.*

YVONNE (*off-screen*): I told him that you weren't in and he said to me "That's all right. I just want to take pictures of Madame Steiner's room." I don't know what else he said after that. That it was for a story, "The Stars at Home," or "In the Privacy of Their Homes . . ."

91. YVONNE (CU *at the door*): I didn't let him in. I told him to call you at the theater. Didn't he call?

92. MARION (*crossing to Yvonne*): No.

YVONNE: Did I do the wrong thing?
MARION: No, Yvonne. You did the right thing. I hate reporters who go snooping around.
YVONNE: Good night, Madame.
MARION: Good night.

Marion closes the door behind Yvonne, then crosses left to the bed, picks up a rolled, tied, bundle of rags, carries it to the door, and lays it against the crack between the door and floor. Crossing left again, she removes her fur coat and spreads it over the bed.

93. Blurred black-and-white shot of one subway train rushing past another.

94 to 99. Alternating reverse-angle shots of Jacquot, watering some plants outside the theater, and Raymond, observing him.

RAYMOND: What are you watering there, Jacquot, flowers?
JACQUOT: They're not flowers.
RAYMOND: Are they vegetables?
JACQUOT: They're not vegetables. You put them in a pipe, you light it, and it makes smoke.
RAYMOND: You know you could wind up in jail. (*He laughs, then looks at his watch.*) Where the hell is she?

100. MS *of Jean-Loup at his desk in the orchestra, the script open before him, making notes. He looks impatiently at his watch, then returns to his writing.*

101. MS *of Arlette from the rear, working on a miniature of the set. Bernard enters from the right and puts his arm around her waist. She brusquely pushes his hand away and glares at him.*

BERNARD (*exasperated*): Oh, it's incredible!
MARION (*off-screen*): Hi. What's going on? Are we rehearsing or not?

102. MS *of Arlette, now from the front, fitting together pieces of the miniature.*

JEAN-LOUP (*off-screen*): We're all set except for Nadine. She'll hear it from me when she gets here.

103. The alley behind the stage door, seen through the open door. A German jeep enters frame, in front of the café across the alley. Nadine jumps out.

RAYMOND (*outside*): Do you know what time it is? You ride around with the jerries and I catch hell.

Nadine and Raymond rush into the theater; camera follows as they hurry toward the stage.

NADINE: I was doing some dubbing. It got late. They offered to give me a ride and I wasn't going to turn it down.
RAYMOND: You're not fussy, are you! If they offered you a role in *Jew Süss* you wouldn't turn it down, either.[9]
NADINE (*having paused and now facing Raymond*): Right you are, sir. Only there are no roles for French women.

104 to 107. Alternating reverse-angle shots of Nadine in ML *range on stage (with other members of the company busy in the background) and of Marion and Jean-Loup in* MC *range seated at the director's table in the orchestra.*

MARION (*off-screen*): We could change the position of the door.
JEAN-LOUP (*off-screen*): Yes, but the door . . .
NADINE: Excuse me, Marion. I'm really sorry.
JEAN-LOUP (*off-screen*): Don't rush. We've only held up the rehearsal for an hour for you. We're not at your service, my dear. What's your excuse today? Didn't your alarm clock go off?
NADINE: No, I was dubbing.
JEAN-LOUP (*off-screen, angrily*): You shouldn't take every job that comes your way. You're working in the theater. Leave the dubbing jobs to your pals who need work.
MARION (*softly, to Jean-Loup*): But she needs work, too.
JEAN-LOUP: Yes, but she's a pain in the ass.

108. Camera, at a somewhat low angle, now slowly moves in on Nadine as she becomes more and more agitated; shot ends in MCU.

NADINE: I'm not leaving work to anybody, and I'm going to accept everything that's offered to me. I do radio broadcasts in the morning, at lunch I do doubling, and in the evening I do walk-ons at the Comédie Française.[10] And every Thursday I play Molière for the schoolchildren. And if someone offers me a bit role in a movie, I say yes. I want to make it. And there's only one way. You have to take everything. You've got to see a lot of people and meet new people all the time. If you want to fire me, go ahead, because Sacha Guitry is holding auditions at the Théâtre Madeleine and I can be there in an hour . . .[11]

109 and 110. Bernard and Christian are seated at a table in the café, seen first through a pane of the café door, then in MC *range. Christian lights a cigarette.*

CHRISTIAN: Did you give some thought to what I asked you?
BERNARD: Yes. And I could only think of two: Raoul Coquet, Fernand Coustal. Do you remember them?
CHRISTIAN (*writing*): Coquet seems a good idea. We'll call him right away. Coustal, I'm not as sure as you, I'll put a question mark by his name. (*He looks outside.*) Is that her?
BERNARD: Yes, it's her.

111. LS, *from point of view of Bernard and Christian, of Marion descending the steps from the stage door; Raymond and Jacquot are at first also in frame. Marion exits left; camera holds on the darkened theater. Marion now moves nervously back into frame, as if planning to reenter the stage door; then she looks toward the café, seems to reconsider, and exits again at frame left.*

CHRISTIAN (*off-screen*): She's still very beautiful.
BERNARD (*off-screen*): Why "still"?
CHRISTIAN (*off-screen*): *The House of Sin* came out the year of my First Communion.
BERNARD (*off-screen*): Did you see *The House of Sin*? How did you manage?
CHRISTIAN (*off-screen*): No, I didn't see it. But I swiped all the stills from the Roxy, including the famous one.
BERNARD (*off-screen*): She's very beautiful . . .

112. Resume on Bernard and Christian as in 110.

BERNARD: . . . but there's something peculiar about her. There's something about that woman I can't figure out. (*He pauses.*)
CHRISTIAN: Come on, let's make the phone call.

As Bernard and Christian rise to leave, camera begins to travel left across other patrons seated against the wall of the café, until it reaches the door; there, through the frame of one pane, we see Marion once more returning to the stage door. She looks again toward the café, but this time decides to enter the stage door. She climbs the stairs, unlocks the door, and slips inside.

113 and 114. Inside the darkened theater. At first, the only fitful illumination is provided by the ray of a flashlight, which finally settles on a large lantern. Removing the lantern from its shelf and striking a match to light it, Marion is fully visible. Picking up the lantern, she makes her way across the stage and through the passageways of the backstage, arriving at last at a trapdoor in Raymond's booth. She hangs the lantern momentarily on the wall, then opens the trapdoor, then places the lantern on the floor and begins to descend. She reaches for the lantern and carries it with her as she shuts the trapdoor behind her. Shot ends in complete darkness. Throughout these shots, Marion's movements seem precise, deliberate, even habitual.

115. CU of the face of Lucas Steiner, suddenly illuminated as he leans forward to light a cigarette with a large candle.

MARION (*off-screen*): Lucas, I have bad news for you.
LUCAS: The Propaganda Office has banned the play.

116 to 119. Alternating CUs of Lucas and Marion.

MARION: No. You can't leave in a week. The lead that I was given is no good.
LUCAS: But you told me it was safe.
MARION: It's never safe. The man who took people across near Nevers was arrested. I may have another solution, but . . . I'm not sure.
LUCAS: Why? Will he be arrested too?

120 to 122. Camera has pulled back somewhat from both Marion and Lucas, but the conversation continues as above.

MARION: No, no. Worse than that. There are guides, so-called guides, who take your money, and then stop their trucks just in front of the Kommandantur.

LUCAS: That way they get paid by both sides. (*He laughs.*)

MARION: And you're not an ordinary client. There are a lot of people who know your face. And then there's your accent . . . No.

123. MLS *of Lucas and Marion that reveals Lucas's den in its original, unadorned state. To the extent that it might be called "furnished," it is with bits and pieces of old theatrical sets and props. Marion's newly acquired ham in its checkered cloth hangs prominently from a hook on one wall.*

Shot begins with Lucas and Marion seated at a table. Marion rises first; Lucas puts on his large black hat, rises, douses his cigarette, and crosses right past Marion, passing out of frame. Marion picks up her coat and lantern and follows him. Lucas in turn grabs some laundry and slop pail. Camera follows them as they proceed generally rightward, toward the spiral staircase that leads to the trapdoor, all the while conversing.

MARION: No. You'll have to resign yourself to spending a number of weeks here. Will you be all right? Will you be able to hold out?

LUCAS: Of course I'll be able to hold out. I'll have to. But I hate feeling useless, paralyzed, trapped. Did you speak with Jean-Loup? Will he help us?

MARION: Listen. I've thought it over. I'd rather not say anything to Jean-Loup. He knows too many people. He goes everywhere, he talks, he fools around. It's too dangerous. Do you know how many letters denouncing the Jews reach the police each day? Give me a guess.

LUCAS: I don't know. Three hundred.

MARION: Fifteen hundred. Fifteen hundred letters a day. "My boss is Jewish." "My neighbor is Jewish." "My father-in-law is Jewish." Everyone thinks you've left. Everyone. It's better to leave things as they are and for me to take care of you by myself.

They have now reached the spiral staircase.

LUCAS (*climbing the stairs behind Marion*): Do you think I let you go first out of politeness? Not at all. I wanted to have a look at your legs.

124 and 125. Marion and Lucas emerge from the trapdoor into Raymond's little booth. The backstage lights are now on.

LUCAS: Mehr licht.[12] I want to take in the smell of the stage.

Lucas crosses the landing to the stage area. He then crosses back to Marion, hands her some of the laundry, and follows her up the stairs to the second floor and then down the corridor. As Lucas enters the bathroom to empty the slop pail, Marion enters the "Administration" offices, where she turns on the light. Through all this, Lucas has been talking virtually without pause.

LUCAS: In my cellar, I know everything that's going on in the theater. In the morning, when the lights dim, I say to myself: "That's it. The rehearsal is beginning." Later, when they go on again, I know that you've gone off to lunch. And then in the evening, when it's dark, I tell myself: "In five minutes Marion will be here." It's the same story as the one in a play I saw in London three years ago. In the evening, the husband made believe he was leaving the house, but almost as soon as the gaslight went down we knew he was in the attic to do God knows what. Do you remember? I almost bought the rights to that property.

Camera holds on the "Administration" door, through which Marion is seen briefly in silhouette, locking it.

126. Marion (*in* MS, *stirring a pot over a burner*): He was very happy at the Grand Guignol. And yet he's very pleased to be here with us. (*Camera follows as she picks up a bread basket and a carafe of wine, crosses right to place them on the table, and then still farther right to the bureau.*) He looks a little like Jean Gabin in *The Human Beast.*[13] Very physical and at the same time very gentle. (*She removes a towel from the top drawer and hands it through a curtain to Lucas in the shower at the right.*) And did you know that he's in the theater because of you?

Marion picks up the laundry; Lucas reaches through the shower doorway and takes it from her.

LUCAS: No, I'll do that myself. Tell me how the work is going.

MARION (*having moved back to the table and lighting a candle*): Jean-Loup is managing very well. Today I was very pleased to see that he is capable of getting very angry.

127. CU *of a telephone.*

MARC (*entering to answer it*): Hello? Good evening, sir. Yes, I'll get him right away.

Marc passes into the next room where Jean-Loup is seated at the dinner table of his handsomely furnished apartment.

MARC: Jean-Loup, it's for you. It's Daxiat.
JEAN-LOUP (*moving to the phone*): What does he want at this hour?
MARC: I don't know.
JEAN-LOUP (*on the phone*): Hello, Daxiat? What's going on?

128. The table in the Théâtre Montmartre offices.

MARION (*entering and beginning to clear the table*): That's all anyone was talking last night about on the last metro. The rehearsals of *The Dead Queen* at the Comédie Française were stopped.[14]
LUCAS (*entering from the right*): Why? Is Montherlant Jewish?
MARION: You're close. (*She crosses left, out of frame, then returns to cross right.*) Daxiat says that very soon he's going to tell the whole truth about the Jews that are still at the Comédie Française. According to Daxiat, Jean Yonnel is a Romanian Jew.[15]

She disappears through the doorway at the right rear.

LUCAS: I don't know if Yonnel is Jewish, half Jewish, or a quarter Jewish. (*He has moved to the right rear doorway.*) What I know is that he should have fled. Fled to the end of the world. Far from the madmen.

Marion has emerged from another door, at the left rear, and crossed right.

LUCAS (*watching her*): They're madmen, do you understand? Madmen. Not only in Germany, but here too. Daxiat and the others. Madmen.

129. Marion's dressing table, on which we see her place a photo of Bernard.

MARION (*off-screen*): Here, you wanted to know what Bernard Granger looks like. Look.
LUCAS (*off-screen*): Perfect. He's perfect. With him, there are no problems. He has a nice goyish face.

Camera moves up from the top of the dressing table to a large mirror. In the mirror we see Lucas and Marion sit on the bed. She lies back, he beside and partly over her. His hand pushes up her skirt and caresses her thigh. They embrace.

MARION: What do you have against goyim?
LUCAS: Nothing. Particularly nothing against those with short skirts and long hair.
MARION: Racist. Dirty racist. My mother always told me that I wouldn't be happy with a Jew. (*She laughs.*)

Fade to black.

130. On stage. Bernard and Nadine are rehearsing. They descend the small staircase built into the set and take fixed positions facing the orchestra.

NADINE: "You know, Carl, if you want to stay in this house, there's a name you must never utter: the name of Charles-Henri." (*Raymond enters and takes the tray that Nadine has been carrying.*) "I had on a new dress last night. Everyone noticed it except you, . . ."

131. MS *of Marion and Jean-Loup at the director's table.*

NADINE (*off-screen*): ". . . you must have been preoccupied."
JEAN-LOUP: That's good, Nadine. That's good. I just want to say one thing: get closer to Bernard at this point. And we're going to give you a lamp . . .

132. Resume on Bernard and Nadine, as in 130.

JEAN-LOUP (*off-screen*): . . . that you will place on the table. That will help you. Raymond, instead of running back and forth . . .

133. Resume on Marion and Jean-Loup, as in 131.

JEAN-LOUP: . . . go get me a lamp.
RAYMOND (*off-screen*): O.K.
JEAN-LOUP: Go on, kids, start again where . . .

134. Resume on Bernard and Nadine, as in 132.

JEAN-LOUP (*off-screen*): . . . you left off.
NADINE: "You're not going to tell me that you have too much work."

135. A door at the rear of the orchestra opens; Daxiat enters.

BERNARD (*off-screen*): "I know, Harriette, that your work is harder than mine."

136. Resume on Jean-Loup and Marion, as in 133; they turn to see who has entered.

BERNARD (*off-screen*): "Some people in this house . . ."

137. Resume on Daxiat, as in 135.

138. Resume on Bernard and Nadine.

BERNARD (*distracted and watching Daxiat entering the auditorium*): . . . should really concern themselves . . ."

139. Daxiat in LS *range walks down the aisle.*

BERNARD (*off-screen*): ". . . only with their own work."

140. Resume on Bernard and Nadine.

NADINE: "Why do you say that to me?"
BERNARD (*out of character, laughing*): Because it's in the script!

Nadine shrugs at Bernard's joke, then looks with interest at Daxiat.

141. Daxiat, as in 139.

142. MCU *of Marion and Jean-Loup at the director's table.*

MARION: It's him, isn't it?
JEAN-LOUP: Yes, it's Daxiat. Go say hello to him. (*He waves at Daxiat.*) Be
   friendly. Don't forget to thank him. After all, he's the one that got us the
   censor's permit.
MARION: O.K., don't worry. Of course I'll thank him.

Marion exits at left: Jean-Loup gestures again to Daxiat.

*143. Daxiat, as in 141. Marion crosses left, then turns up the aisle and extends
her hand to Daxiat, who kisses it.*

JEAN-LOUP (*off-screen*): We'll break for a couple of minutes. Take advantage
   of it to relax.
MARION (*to Daxiat*): Good afternoon.
DAXIAT: Good afternoon, Madame Steiner.

144. MCU *of Nadine and Bernard on stage, Raymond behind and between
them.*

BERNARD: Who is that guy?
RAYMOND: Don't you know him? He's the Inspector General. Daxiat, the
   reviewer for *Je suis partout.*
NADINE: Is that Daxiat? That's not how I imagined he'd look. I'd like to meet
   him.
BERNARD: You're not fussy, are you!
NADINE: He's very important. He may soon be the director of the Comédie
   Française.

*145 to 151. Marion and Daxiat in close range, first in alternating over-the-
shoulder shots, then each alone in* CU.

DAXIAT: I want to tell you something that may seem odd to you coming from
   me. But I think that your husband, Lucas Steiner, was wrong in leaving

France. The recent law against Israelites in the theater concerns speculators and profiteers.[16] But your husband, Madame Steiner, was a rare pearl. He was the only Israelite theater director—

MARION: You may say "Jewish."

DAXIAT: —yes, who was at the same time an administrator, a director, and an artist. You see, the Germans are very committed to culture, very. They don't want talent to leave France. As for your play, *The Vanished One*, I am not at all worried about it. I'm certain Jean-Loup Cottins is equal to the challenge.

152. Camera follows Germaine as she hurries down the steps from the stage and up the aisle toward Daxiat and Marion.

DAXIAT (*off-screen*): Naturally, one might ask why this play, which even Pitoëff turned down, was chosen.[17]

Germaine has reached Marion's side and whispers a question.

MARION: All right. (*Marion presents Germaine to Daxiat.*) Do you know Germaine Fabre, my dresser? She has been with me for a very long time. She has something to ask you.

DAXIAT: Yes, of course I know her. Hello.

GERMAINE: It's about my son, Pierre.

Meanwhile, camera follows as Marion crosses right and rejoins Jean-Loup in the set-up of 142.

MARION: What is Daxiat doing here?

JEAN-LOUP: He likes to sniff around rehearsals like this when he's interested in the play.

MARION: Will he write about us?

JEAN-LOUP: I don't know. He either will or won't.

MARION: I wish he would forget about us.

JEAN-LOUP: I'll go see him.

MARION: No, no, stay here.

153. Germaine and Daxiat in MS range. She is pointing to a folder filled with documents, which she flips through.

GERMAINE: Look. We're all good Catholics in our family. Here's the proof.
DAXIAT: Very well. (*He takes the folder.*) I'll take good care of this.

He crosses left.

GERMAINE: Thank you.

154. Camera follows Daxiat as he ascends the steps to the stage, followed by Jean-Loup.

JEAN-LOUP: I'd like to introduce you to our little company.
DAXIAT: All right.

They walk to the center of the stage, where the participants in the production are assembled.

JEAN-LOUP: This is Nadine Marsac, who is, in my view, the best student of the Simon studio. She plays Harriette.

155. Marion (*approaching Germaine in the aisle*): So?

GERMAINE: He was very kind. He took my file.

Marion, smiling, turns to look at the stage.

156. Continues 154. Daxiat crosses steadily left on the stage. Hand extended, he approaches Bernard, who quickly steps back.

JEAN-LOUP: Bernard Granger, our leading man, fresh out of the Grand Guignol—as you will notice.
DAXIAT: Does he play Carl?
JEAN-LOUP: Yes.

Bernard continues to retreat. He steps up a few stairs into the doorway of the half-constructed set, and proceeds to hang monkeylike from the frame.

DAXIAT: I would have imagined him more readily in *The Hairy Ape*.[18]

JEAN-LOUP: Yes, er . . . and Raymond, who will show you out.
NADINE (*approaching Jean-Loup*): Doesn't he like women, your Daxiat?

157. Camera follows Daxiat in MS *range crossing left through the backstage area and toward the stage door, followed by Raymond.*

RAYMOND: Monsieur Daxiat, may I ask you a trick question?
DAXIAT: A trick question?
RAYMOND: Yes, a trick question. (*He removes a pole from against the wall.*) What do you call this?
DAXIAT: A fishing rod.
RAYMOND: That's it. Or a *gaule*. But (*reaching for a second pole*) if I put another next to it, than I have *deux gaules*.[19]
DAXIAT: Bravo, Raymond. (*He passes through the stage door, turns around to look back at Raymond.*) You are very witty.

Raymond slams the door after Daxiat.

158. Bernard and Christian seen through a window frame at a table in the café, talking; we do not hear their words.

159. The Offices of Je sui partout. *Daxiat stands before a microphone. Camera moves in slowly as he speaks.*

DAXIAT: I give my weekly address here before the printing presses of this modest newspaper that will continue to shout the truth. Yes, the French theater must be purged of Jews from the rafters to the prompter's box. If we allow one Jewish prompter to remain in the musical theater of Ménilmontant, we run the risk of finding him some day controlling the destiny of the Opéra.[20] The Jew must be pushed off the stage, out of the wings. He must never be allowed on again. A Jew must never again own, or direct, or administer a theater because all Jews who have been in that position have brought to it their devious and dirty methods. Let these gentlemen be warned: France is off limits to Jews.

160. CU *of a radio. Camera pulls back, revealing Marion seated at her desk, Merlin standing beside her at the left.*

Daxiat's voice continues: And doesn't that mean that for Frenchmen, France is three quarters of the way to salvation?

Marion reaches over to switch off the radio.

MERLIN: This is what you requested, Madame Steiner. I've checked. It's all here. But if you need as much every month, it won't be easy.

Camera follows Merlin as he crosses left to the door.

MARION (*off-screen*): Who said anything about every month? This is altogether exceptional.
MERLIN (*opening the door*): In that case, there's no problem. Good-bye.
MARION (*off-screen*): Good-bye.

Through the doorway, we see Rosette, who wears the yellow Star of David with the word "Jew" on her chest, and Arlette. Passing through, Merlin shakes Arlette's hand and greets her.

ARLETTE: Hello, Monsieur Merlin. (*She takes Rosette by the shoulders.*) Go on in. (*She sees Marion, who has entered at frame right.*) Marion, I'd like you to meet Rosette.
MARION: Hello, Rosette.
ROSETTE: Hello.
ARLETTE: Rosette, you put your samples on the desk and go home.

Rosette crosses right to the desk; Marion follows her.

MARION: How old are you, Rosette?
ROSETTE: I'll be fourteen in three months.
MARION: You work with Arlette? So you're no longer in school?
ROSETTE: I didn't want to go anymore.
MARION: Do you like making costumes?

161. MS of Arlette in the clothes closet.

ROSETTE (*off-screen*): Yes, Madame.

MARION (*off-screen*): Will you come see the play?
ARLETTE: Look, Marion, she can't go to the theater. (*She points to her own chest where the Star of David might be affixed.*) The kid can't go out in the evening.

162. Resume on Marion and Rosette.

ROSETTE: Yes, I can go out in the evening. Three months ago someone gave me a ticket. I heard Edith Piaf at the ABC.[21] I put my scarf like this. (*She adjusts the scarf to cover the star.*) The bottom tucked into my belt. It worked out very well.

163. ARLETTE (CU): We'll talk about it later. Go home, Rosette. Do you know what time it is?

164. Resume on Marion and Rosette as in 162.

ROSETTE (*crossing toward the door*): Good-bye Madame.
MARION: Good-bye.

Marion looks with concern at Rosette as she exits.

165 to 169. Series of shots showing Marion and Arlette closing up the office for the evening, putting on their fur coats, and departing.

ARLETTE: You have funny ideas sometimes, Marion. The girl won't forget. She'll want to come see the play. And since her parents can't say no to her, they'll complain to me.
MARION: Excuse me. I'm sorry. I wanted to be nice to this girl on account of . . . Are her parents French?
ARLETTE: The girl was born in Paris but her parents are Polish. Her father is a tailor. He works at home—that is, in the attic. The daughter makes deliveries because he can't go out in the street. His accent is so thick, you can cut it with a knife.
MARION (*with heightened interest*): An accent like Lucas's?
ARLETTE: Much stronger than Lucas's. And he hardly knows thirty words of French. If a German asked for directions in the street, that would be it. So he shuts himself up in the house. His wife does everything.

MARION: Isn't he afraid someone will denounce him? Doesn't he want to get to the Free Zone?
ARLETTE: Naturally he wants to leave. But you know, it costs an arm and a leg, and these people have no money.

As they leave, Marion extinguishes the light and closes the "Administration" door.

170. Marion and Arlette descend the stairs past Raymond's booth, pausing outside the booth to finish their conversation.

ARLETTE: What are you doing tonight?
MARION: Nothing special. I'm going home.
ARLETTE: I'm inviting you to dinner.
MARION: I'm terribly sorry. I can't.
ARLETTE: But after all, Marion, you can't spend all your evenings alone like this.
MARION: I have to go home. I'm off.

Marion enters the booth and reaches for the light switch; the screen goes black.

171. The cellar. Shot opens on Lucas, in left profile in MS *range, holding up a pile of manuscripts.*

LUCAS: I've read all of these, Madame Manager. There's nothing in here for us. (*He turns left; camera follows him as he crosses left to a table and stops beside Marion as she folds clothes and places them in a traveling bag. Lucas lays the scripts on the table.*) You had better send them back. And don't forget to remove my reader's notes and burn them. They're in my handwriting, after all.
MARION: Yes, of course. I'll see to it. I have to explain the matter of the money to you. (*Camera follows as she crosses right to pick up her purse from the bed and then returns to the table.*) I've prepared three packets of bills. The first is for the conveyor who will take you to Vierzon.

She removes three wads of bills from the purse and shows them to Lucas.

LUCAS: Conveyor? Is that what they're called?

He begins to cross left.

MARION: Yes, conveyors. You have to pay him as soon as you get on the truck. (*She has turned to face Lucas, who has taken his place at frame left.*) He promised me you would be comfortable. It's a moving van. You'll be in the midst of furniture.

LUCAS (*grandly crossing his arms*): I'll be sitting in an armchair, like a prime minister.

MARION: Please, Lucas, listen to me carefully. This is serious. The second packet is for the farmer who will take you across the demarcation line. He has the good fortune to own a large piece of property that straddles the border. One end is in the Free Zone.

LUCAS (*who has crossed back right, close to Marion*): Let me guess. The third packet is for Spain.

MARION: Yes, for Spain, and also for the rest. And since this won't be enough, I've brought a little bag . . .

Camera follows as she crosses right and takes a small bag from her coat pocket. Lucas has followed her; she turns and holds the bag up to him. He reaches inside and finds jewels.

LUCAS: No, Madame. Not the jewels. (*He takes the bag from her and tosses it back on her coat.*) Not the jewels!

MARION: You may need them.

LUCAS: Less than you will. You'll bring them with you when you join me. (*Marion crosses left behind Lucas toward the head of the bed.*) I want you to come join me . . . as soon as possible.

Marion picks up a stool from beside the bed and walks toward camera, crossing past Lucas who has moved to frame left. She puts the stool down next to a small table on which sits a radio.

MARION: Certainly, but to keep up appearances I have to play the first hundred performances at least.

LUCAS: My God, what confidence! (*He strikes his head. Marion, behind him, puts her hands on his shoulders and pushes him down on the stool.*) You think the play will run for a hundred performances? That will take six

months. (*Marion crosses right, picks up a folding leather make-up case, returns with it, and places it on the table at frame left.*) I want you to come after the fiftieth. No later.

MARION (*removing a towel from the case*): All right, after the fiftieth I'll say I have a spot on my lung and I'll get someone to replace me. (*She tucks the towel into Lucas's collar.*) I'll explain the situation to Jean-Loup. Then I'll hand over the management of the theater to him and make as if I were leaving for a sanatorium. I'll join you wherever you are.

During the last few moments of the shot, "Mon Amant de Saint-Jean," the song heard over the credits, appears on the soundtrack, now coming from the radio.

172. CU *of Lucas, Marion behind him, her arms on his shoulders. The song on the soundtrack becomes more prominent.*

LUCAS: And we'll have a new start.

He kisses her left hand; with her right hand she strokes his neck.

173 to 182. Series of alternating CUS *of Lucas, as in 171, and of Marion as she cuts his hair. The only brief camera movement occurs when Lucas first reaches into the make-up case. Lucas removes a huge hooked false nose from the case and places it over his own.*

MARION: I'm not a hairdresser. Stop fidgeting. I can't do it this way. (*She sees the false nose on Lucas's face.*) My God, Lucas, that's awful.
LUCAS (*looking at himself in a hand mirror he has taken from the case*): I'm trying to feel Jewish. Playing the Jew is very tricky. If you underplay they say you're exaggerating; if you overplay, they say you don't look Jewish. What does it mean to look Jewish?
MARION: You're asking *me*? Stop fidgeting.
LUCAS (*removing the false nose and pausing*): Listen, Marion, listen.

He turns toward the radio.

183. CU *of radio as Lucas turns up the volume.*

184 to 188. Again, a series of alternating CUS *of Lucas and Marion.*

LUCAS: I love this song.

Lucas does indeed listen with particular attention to the song throughout these shots. The song differs from the version heard over the credits in that it now concludes with the following stanza:

> And I, who loved him so,
> My beautiful love, my handsome lover of Saint-Jean;
> He no longer loves me.
> It's in the past; let's speak of it no more.
> He no longer loves me.
> It's in the past; let's speak of it no more.

Just before the words "He no longer loves me," *Lucas nods with a fleeting smile.*

189. A still closer shot of Marion. She too is now clearly noticing the words of the song, and she looks at the radio most pointedly at the last repetition of the phrase "It's in the past."

190. Camera follows Jean-Loup as he exits from the stage door, walks down the steps and past Jacquot, who is watering his garden.

JEAN-LOUP: How's the garden going?
JACQUOT: Fine.
JEAN-LOUP: Is it growing?
JACQUOT: Sure is.
JEAN-LOUP: So, soon we'll have a smoke.

Jean-Loup continues his walk, away from camera, pauses, turns around, and returns toward Jacquot.

JEAN-LOUP: Say, Jacquot, will you come here for a moment?

Jacquot moves a few steps toward Jean-Loup.

191. MS of Jacquot and Jean-Loup.

JEAN-LOUP: Listen, Jacquot.

JACQUOT: Yes?
JEAN-LOUP: Can you repeat a sentence after me?

192. MCS of Jacquot, looking up at Jean-Loup.

JACQUOT: Yes.
JEAN-LOUP: Will you do it?
JACQUOT: Sure.
JEAN-LOUP: Good. Try saying "Mother, do you think Monsieur Carl will
   return?"
JACQUOT: "Mother, do you think Monsieur Carl will return?"
JEAN-LOUP: That's good. And then: "Because I learn a lot with him."
JACQUOT: "Because I learn a lot with him."

*193. Low angle shot of Jean-Loup, seen over Jacquot's shoulder. Jean-Loup
smiles, begins to turn away, mutters a word of approval, and exits at frame
right.*

*194. The square in front of the theater. Marion enters from frame left. Camera
follows her as she walks along the street, nodding to a female passerby and
then coming upon a small crowd of people listening to a street singer and
accordionist. They are performing "Mon Amant de Saint-Jean." Marion
passes behind them and out of frame right. In a moment, she reenters frame,
approaching the crowd. She gestures to the child who is selling copies of the
song, reaches into her bag, pays for a copy, and begins to examine it. She
turns and once again moves toward frame right. This time camera follows her
somewhat farther, past a German soldier seated at an easel working on a
painting of Sacré-Coeur; Marion again exits frame right.*[22]

*195. Marion continues her walk toward the stage door. Entering at left in ML
range, she turns the corner and walks along the length of the theater as
Jacquot comes toward her.*

MARION: Hello, Jacquot.
JACQUOT: "Mother, is Monsieur Carl going to return?"
MARION: Why do you say that to me?
JACQUOT: "Because I work well with him."

MARION: What are you saying?
JACQUOT (*pointing toward camera*): He told me to say that to you.

196. Jean-Loup in CS *peeps out impishly from behind a building, then retreats.*

197. Resume on Marion and Jacquot.

MARION: "He" who?
JACQUOT (*continuing to point*): Him, over there.

198. Jean-Loup, as in 196. He shrugs his shoulders.

199. CU *of Marion, laughing.*

200. The stage, seen now from a low angle; the set continues to take shape. Jean-Loup, in LS, *is directing a scene, standing at the right of the doorway of the set.*

RAYMOND (*testing the door*): O.K., there, now it works.
JEAN-LOUP: And a good thing, too. Nadine, are you ready?
NADINE (*off-screen*): Yes. (*She enters and closes the door behind her. Camera follows as she walks left, passing Bernard in the background, to the table where Marion and Jacquot are seated, facing front.*) "Do you need me any more, Madame? May I go and prepare Eric's room?"
MARION: "I wish you would, Harriette. And don't forget the pomade for his left hand."

Nadine continues to walk left.

JACQUOT: "I'm finished, Mother."
MARION: "That's fine, Eric. Go off to bed now."

Jean-Loup enters frame and moves left to the table. Camera follows as he directs Jacquot, who rises from the table, toward the stairway of the set (at the top of which stands Germaine), then back toward the table to face Marion.

JEAN-LOUP: Walk to the stairs, up to the door. There we are. When you reach

the second step, turn around. Don't trip, step in this spot and deliver your
lines.
JACQUOT: "Mother, is Monsieur Carl going to return?"
MARION: "I don't know, my child. What do you think?"
JACQUOT: "I think he is going to return. I learn well with him."

*Jacquot turns, runs off to the left as Germaine crosses past him, down a few
steps. Jean-Loup follows Jacquot, lifts him up, carries him to center stage, and
puts him down. Nadine, Bernard, and Raymond have grouped behind Marion.*

JEAN-LOUP: Good, very good, Jacquot. Bravo, Jacquot. Well, now we know
there will be at least one good actor in this play.

Nadine, Bernard, and Marion protest good-naturedly in unison.

201. Raymond in MS *left profile dominates the frame as first Germaine and
then Arlette enter from the left to kiss him and say good night. As Arlette kisses
Raymond, Bernard enters at frame right.*

BERNARD: So he gets a kiss, and I . . .
ARLETTE (*reaching across Raymond to Bernard*): You get a handshake.
BERNARD (*refusing to release Arlette's hand*): Since you absolutely refuse,
may I? I'd like to read your palm. Let's see. There are two women in you.
ARLETTE: Yes, but unfortunately neither of them cares to sleep with you. Bye
bye.

*Arlette exits through the doorway in center frame. Bernard moves to follow her,
then pauses, framed in the doorway, now shifting his attention between Arlette
(off-screen) and Raymond.*

BERNARD: It's my fault. It's my fault. I shouldn't have let on so soon that I
wanted her. Now she needles me, she provokes me. When the sets and the
costumes are finished, she's going to disappear from my life. (*He clenches
his fist.*) I simply have to make it with this woman before the dress rehearsal!

He unclenches his fist and strikes his chest in frustration.

202. Camera follows Raymond as he rushes into Marion's offices on the second floor, where Martine, Marion, and Nadine are examining some clothing, presumably from the black market, spread out on a table.

MARION (*off-screen*): Do you have my size in beige, by any chance?
RAYMOND (*reaching the group and speaking angrily to Martine*): What are you doing there? Stop bothering Madame Steiner!
MARION: She's not bothering me, Raymond. Please go. It's all right.
RAYMOND: O.K.

He exits at frame right.

MARTINE (*to Marion*): When I get some in size three, I'll bring them over.
MARION (*reaching down to the table to pick up a stocking*): Aren't you going to buy any, Nadine?
NADINE: I'd like to, but I don't have the money.
MARION: You're joking, surely.

She looks down at Nadine's legs.

NADINE: No.

203. Shot of table top, to which first Nadine, then Martine lift their legs to display them to Marion while their voices continue on the soundtrack.

NADINE: I use make-up on my legs.
MARTINE: Me, too. This is make-up.
NADINE: Yes, but you're much more chic. You draw the seam.
MARION: How elegant!

204. CU of Marion.

MARTINE (*off-screen*): The seam is drawn with a pen. It has to be straight. It's really much safer to have someone else do it.
NADINE (*off-screen*): A man, preferably.

Marion's eye has fallen on the newspaper lying on the table, on which Martine had placed her foot.

205. CU *of newspaper headline:* "GERMAN TROOPS CROSS LINE OF DEMARCATION." *The newspaper is dated "Thursday, 12 November 1942."*

206. Resume CU *of Marion, who looks left, then right.*

MARION: What is this? Is it today's paper? (*She reads, then turns in the direction of Martine.*) Did you know that the Free Zone had been invaded?
MARTINE (*off-screen*): It was announced this morning on the radio.
NADINE (*off-screen*): This doesn't change anything. Do you think the Free Zone will be . . .

The voices of Martine and Nadine are covered by soundtrack music as camera holds on Marion.

207. The cellar. CU *of Lucas, who almost at once begins to move to the right, followed by camera.*

LUCAS: The Free Zone has been invaded? I don't see how that makes any difference. You would have had me cross half of France while it was full of Germans; well, now I'll just cross the whole of France.

Lucas has moved into a two-shot set-up with Marion, who stands at frame right before a table, unpacking Lucas's traveling bag.

MARION: You won't cross anything at all. The Germans are everywhere. Every single truck is stopped and searched every fifty kilometers. And I spoke with my contact. He's scared to death. He doesn't even want to hear about it anymore. No, no. This kind of escape has become too dangerous for everyone.
LUCAS (*having crossed behind Marion and now standing to the right of her*): So? What happens to me in the meantime?
MARION: You'll stay here until things calm down.
LUCAS: I can't stay here anymore or I'll go crazy. This is no life. (*He begins shaking a book at Marion.*) Have you ever asked yourself what I do here

all day? I read and I read. I read a lot. (*He puts the book down and walks to the right.*) I listen to lies on the radio. Then I read lies in the press. (*He is now standing between the radio and a table laden with books.*) And to keep my brain from addling, I pick up the crossword puzzle. (*He picks up a newspaper from the table.*) Do you want to see my crossword puzzle? Here. "Symbol of lowliness," in six letters: "HEBREW." In the other direction, in eight letters, "Stinking carcasses": "SHEENIES." (*He drops the paper and picks up a small book.*) And these are for children. "We can never be sufficiently suspicious of them," in four letters.

208. CU *reaction shot of Marion.*

LUCAS (*continuing, off-screen*): It begins with a "J". So, I put down the crossword puzzle and I listen to the sounds of the theater. I strain for your steps . . .

209. Resume on Lucas.

LUCAS: . . . on the staircase, I wait for you to come. (*He begins to cross left, followed by camera.*) I wait and I wait. (*Frame now includes Marion at the left. Lucas has begun to scream.*) I've had enough of waiting! How long does a man have to live? (*He turns to the wall and begins to weep. Marion moves to him.*) I can't stand it anymore, Marion. (*She strokes his back.*) I can't stand it anymore.

He continues to weep. Then he removes his coat from its hook on the wall.

MARION: Listen, Lucas. Lucas.
LUCAS: I'm leaving.
MARION: Where are you going?
LUCAS: I'm getting out of here. I'm leaving. I'm going to talk to them.

He now faces Marion and begins to put on his scarf.

MARION: What are you saying?
LUCAS: To City Hall. To police headquarters. I'll explain to them. I'll register. I'll get my papers in order.

MARION: Have you gone crazy? (*Lucas pulls away from her; she grabs desperately at his coat.*) What are you doing? (*She continues to hang on to him; he pulls her with him as he moves, walking backwards to the left.*) You're not leaving here! (*Marion has crossed in front of Lucas and now stands at frame left facing him, still holding on to his coat.*) What is it you want? A concentration camp? Is that what you want?

LUCAS: Let me pass! Let me pass!

MARION (*retreating as Lucas advances*): You're not leaving. I'll crack your skull!

They are now in close range beneath a shelf, from which Marion grabs a miniature column; she smashes Lucas over the head with it. We hear him fall to the floor. Marion, in CU, *retreats in horror into a shadow, places her hands before her face, and shuts her eyes; then, in profile, she steps forward into the light and, her hands still covering her face up to the eyes, she looks downward to the floor.*

210. CU *of Lucas. Camera pulls back enough to show us Marion putting a glass to his lips.*

MARION: Here. It's real cognac. Good cognac from the black market.

LUCAS: You're trembling. You need a glass of cognac, too.

MARION: I just discovered something awful about myself. I'm capable of killing a man. (*Lucas touches her cheek.*) We're going to fix up this cellar. I'll bring you a good bed, a comfortable armchair. And some rugs to cover the floor.

LUCAS: I need a work table.

MARION: Yes. Just like an apartment.

LUCAS: I hope you won't forget to cover the walls with flowered paper.

Marion smiles and bends to kiss Lucas. She tilts her head backwards until her crown of upswept hair dominates the screen.

Fade to black.

211 to 214. The next morning. CU *of Lucas and Marion still asleep, her head on his shoulder. Marion awakens to sounds of activity in the theater above.*

Marion is then seen peering out of the trapdoor; a brief shot of Merlin, in silhouette behind a door pane, is intercut.

MARC (*off-screen*): Madame Steiner wants the gamekeeper to have a rifle.
MERLIN (*off-screen*): But Madame Steiner doesn't realize that even for a prop rifle you need a permit. If she thinks it's easy to get one . . .
MARC (*off-screen*): But that's what she told me.

215. The cellar.

MARION (*descending the spiral staircase from the trap door*): I can't go out that way. They're all here already. (*Having reached the bottom of the staircase, she pauses to speak with Lucas.*) We should know better. We should have gotten up earlier.
LUCAS: So go out through the little alley.
MARION: That's right.

She retreats toward the back door of the cellar.

LUCAS: Marion?
MARION: Yes?
LUCAS: Don't forget to lock the door behind you.
MARION: O.K.

216. High angle shot of Marion emerging from the cellar door and locking it. Camera pulls back as she ascends the outside cellar steps, then follows her progress into the building and down a corridor.
Meanwhile, the soundtrack picks up a conversation between Germaine and Raymond.

GERMAINE (*off-screen*): I had word from my oldest. They sent him to another stalag. He's not allowed to tell me where he is.

217 to 220. The conversation between Raymond and Germaine runs over all the action. First we see a table top on which Raymond and Germaine are making an exchange: she gives him a pair of gloves, he passes her a set of small boxes of tobacco. The camera lifts to hold on Raymond and Germaine in MS range. Intercut is first a brief shot of Marion, still stealing silently through the backstage passageways towards her office, later a shot of Bernard entering and briefly toying with a phonograph as he passes on his way toward Raymond and Germaine.

GERMAINE: I won't put them all in the same package. That way there's a better chance that one will get through.
RAYMOND (*putting on the gloves*): They fit me perfectly. I guess I'm the same size as your husband.
GERMAINE: He wasn't my husband. He was my number two man . . . I bet you can't guess where I got them: at the Colonial Exposition.[23] I had to pay dearly for them . . . He and I weren't together for long. He was left-handed.
RAYMOND: You have something against left-handed people?
GERMAINE: No, but then when he slapped me I didn't have a chance to see it coming. We had some good times, and some damned awful ones.

221. Raymond and Germaine, still in MS range, continue to talk as Bernard joins them. Bernard enters right, moves behind and between Raymond and Germaine and kisses Germaine.

BERNARD: Hello.
RAYMOND: Hello, Bernard.
BERNARD: Hello, Raymond.
GERMAINE: Hello, Bernard. For God's sake, didn't you sleep at home last
    night? Your beard scratches.
BERNARD: No, I didn't sleep at home.

*222. Marion is ascending the stairs to the "Administration" offices. At
Bernard's last words, she pauses briefly and turns her head.*

*223. Resume on Raymond, Bernard, and Germaine. Bernard moves left, then
crosses right as he recounts this tale to the others.*

BERNARD: I had a close call. When the movie let out last night, there was a
    raid for "Voluntary Labor for Germany." Two guys blocked the door and
    started checking everyone. So I turned my head in one direction (*he stiffens
    his back and looks over his right shoulder, nose in air*) and my body in the
    other (*he repeats his gesture*) so that each of them thought the other had
    checked me out.
GERMAINE: (*crossing past Bernard to the right*): If I were you I wouldn't brag
    about that kind of thing. It's because of guys like you that they don't let the
    prisoners come home.

224. CU *of Germaine entering the "Administration" door. She crosses left past
Marion in* MS *range in the bathroom. Camera holds on Marion, who is removing
her blouse.*

MARION: Hello, Germaine.
GERMAINE: Hello. What's going on? You get dressed in the theater these
    days?
MARION: You don't have to shout it from the rooftops. That's right. I didn't
    sleep at home last night.

225. CU *of Germaine as she turns to look with lifted brows at Marion.*

226. MLS *of Bernard being fitted for a costume. A tailor circles him, taking his
measurements and announcing them in Italian to Arlette, who, seated at the*

right repeats them (in Italian) and notes them down on a pad. Raymond,
carrying a prop, crosses in the foreground.

BERNARD: I can't stand to have a man touch me, Arlette. Couldn't you take
   his place, please?
ARLETTE: How come you don't ask me how I feel about it? What if I hate to
   touch men? (*She laughs.*)

Bernard stares at Arlette; she rises, moves a few paces left, and returns, still
laughing, to stand beside Bernard.

BERNARD: You haven't forgotten my second costume, have you?
ARLETTE (*taken aback*): Is there a second costume?
BERNARD (*pointing to the script in his hand*): That's what it says in the script.
   Act two, scene three: "Carl enters wearing a stealthy look." I need a stealthy
   look to put on.

Arlette sniffs at Bernard's joke; Bernard, looking pleased with himself, again
faces front.

227. *Outside the stage door stands Christian in* MLS. *He looks at his watch,*
then, cautiously, at a passing German soldier. He pauses a moment; camera
follows as he crosses the alley to the open window of the concierge's flat, at
which sits Jacquot.

CHRISTIAN: Do you know Bernard Granger?
JACQUOT: He's the new actor.
CHRISTIAN: Yes. Tell him I couldn't wait. Give him this package. From
   Christian.
JACQUOT: I'll give it to him.

228. *Shot opens on the spiral staircase to the cellar. Marion slowly descends,*
then crosses left to the bed, where she places her purse, tossing her fur coat on
a chair. We see that the cellar has been considerably altered: a new bed, a
large ornamental screen, and so forth, are beginning to give it the air of the
"apartment" that Marion promised in 210. A Spanish-style song, "Sombréros
et Mantilles," sung in French, is heard very loud on the soundtrack.

MARION: Lucas? Lucas? Lucas! Lucas!

LUCAS (*off-screen*): Marion? Marion, are you there?

MARION: Where are you?

LUCAS (*off-screen*): Stand by my bed. Say something.

MARION: What should I say? I'm right by your bed.

LUCAS (*off-screen*): I can't hear you very well.

MARION: I can't hear you well, either.

LUCAS (*off-screen*): Go stand near the radio.

MARION (*looking all around*): Where is the radio? I hear it but I don't see it.

LUCAS (*off-screen*): It's near the boiler.

MARION: Near the boiler? (*She crosses right, turns the corner, and moves left toward the radio.*) Here I am. (*She notices a plugged hole in the flue above the radio. She removes the plug and speaks into the hole.*) Is this how you hear?

LUCAS (*off-screen*): Just as if you were right next to me. Turn the radio up louder and come up to the stage.

Marion turns the radio dial and passes right to exit frame.

229. The theater wings, directly off the stage. Marion enters left, and descends from the landing toward camera. The "Spanish" song continues on the soundtrack, as it will for the next three shots.

MARION (*in CS range, looking downward*): My God, this is very dangerous.

230. CU of the floor, where Lucas is removing tiles. Camera lifts to a profile shot of Lucas, in his black hat, kneeling.

LUCAS: On the contrary, it's wonderful. This is the old heating vent. That means that if I can improve the system a little . . .

231. Reaction shot of Marion, still looking downward.

LUCAS (*off-screen*): . . . I can hear down below everything that's going on up here. I can follow the rehearsals at last.

232. Resume on Lucas, as in 230.

LUCAS: Every night as long as rehearsals go on I'll tell you what you should suggest to Jean-Loup so that he can tell the actors. (*Camera follows his movement as he rises to his feet.*) Of course *The Vanished One* will run for a hundred performances. (*His gestures betray a growing excitement. He walks left, then back to Marion as camera follows.*) *The Vanished One* will run for a year. I'm back in business! I'm running my theater again! I'm directing the play! And no one will ever figure it out.

Now facing a smiling Marion, he begins to stamp his heels in time with the "Spanish" song. He takes Marion in his arms and dances her in circles to the left. As the song comes to an end, he repeats the last syllables and strikes a flamenco pose, hand over head.

233. On stage. Bernard enters the left foreground in CU *range. Camera pulls back to reveal Bernard, Marion, and Jean-Loup in* MS *range, rehearsing; Jean-Loup guides Marion, then Bernard, to the position he desires.*

BERNARD: "Since I set foot in this house all I've heard is lies. And these lies contradict one another terribly."
MARION: "They're not lies. They are lapses of memory." (*After Jean-Loup shifts her position on the stage, she repeats the lines.*) "They're not lies. They are lapses of memory. For years, I've been the one who has sought the truth."

In a single unbroken movement, camera (1) follows Jean-Loup as he walks to the apron of the stage and steps over the footlights, down toward Marc who sits at the director's table in the orchestra, (2) tracks the length of the apron along the footlights, past the curtain and into the wings, and (3) lowers to a CS *of the heating vent. The voices of Marion and Bernard continue on the soundtrack.*

MARION (*off-screen*): "Don't you understand how awful it is not to know who one is, what one has done? And to live in terror that it will happen again. Sometimes, I have the sense that I don't really exist."
BERNARD (*off-screen*): "Why has Doctor Sanders never allowed you to go to town? Or consult another doctor?"

234. The tracking movement begun in 233 seems to continue uninterrupted past this cut: camera moves slowly down the flue to the hole in the wall, to the left of which Lucas, now wearing his spectacles, carefully listens to the play.

MARION (*off-screen*): "He knows more than all the other doctors. Without him I would be dead. My entire life will not be time enough to express my gratitude."

BERNARD (*off-screen, very loudly*): "The prisoner owes no gratitude to the jailer! And Doctor Sanders has made you his prisoner. If someone says to you quite simply 'Helena, I love you' . . ."

235. Bernard and Marion in ML range on stage, facing the orchestra.

BERNARD: ". . . why not listen to him?"

Marion begins to speak, but hesitates over her next line.

BERNARD (*interrupting her*): No. I'm sorry. I'm sorry. Excuse me. (*Bernard walks toward camera and addresses Jean-Loup directly.*) Do we really have to shout through this whole dialogue, Jean-Loup? I . . . really, I don't know. It just doesn't seem right to me. (*He casts his eyes upward despairingly.*) It sounds wrong.

236. Marc and Jean-Loup at the director's table.

JEAN-LOUP (*pointing to a pile of papers before him*): But look, Bernard, Lucas's notes are quite explicit. Listen to this: "This scene must be played like a duel."

237. Resume on Bernard.

BERNARD: Like a duel.

He sighs and turns away.

238. Bernard, back to camera, walks upstage toward Marion, who moves a few paces downstage.

BERNARD: All right. But it seems strange to me. (*He steps back into character.*) "The prisoner owes no gratitude to the jailer." (*Bernard crosses behind Marion, then back to frame left, gesturing.*) "And Doctor Sanders has made you his prisoner. If someone says to you quite simply 'Helena, I love you,' why not listen to him?"

MARION: "But I don't have the right to love, don't you understand? Neither to love nor to be loved."

BERNARD: "No, Helena, no!" (*He crosses behind her.*) "Those are Doctor Sanders's words. I'm going to tell you something about Doctor Sanders." (*He pauses, then turns to Jean-Loup.*) There. (*He moves toward camera.*) You told me to shout so I shouted. But playing this scene that way just doesn't seem right to me.

MARION (*also moving toward camera*): To me neither, Jean-Loup. This scene doesn't seem right. You see, it doesn't seem right to us.

She glances slyly at Bernard.

239. The cellar. MCU *of Lucas, drinking coffee.*

LUCAS: Bernard Granger is correct. This scene should not be shouted.

Camera moves back to reveal the whole table, Marion seated at the left.

MARION: Now listen. Jean-Loup was only following your directions.

She rises, removes the dishes from the table, and crosses left to a sideboard.

LUCAS: Yes, but I make mistakes from time to time. And Jean-Loup shouldn't stick so closely to my notes.

The lamp hanging over the table suddenly goes out; the next few lines are spoken in darkness.

LUCAS: What is it?
MARION: There must be a power failure. It's the electricity.
LUCAS (*striking a match*): Will you pass me the candle?
MARION (*thinking*): Candle, candle . . .

The light suddenly returns.

MARION (*scraping dishes*): Here it is. The light is back.
LUCAS (*still holding the lit match and looking for a cigarette on the table*): This scene must not be played like a duel but like a conspiracy. (*He lights the cigarette.*) Am I boring you, Marion? You're not listening to me.
MARION: I'm sorry, Lucas. I'm dead tired.
LUCAS: Well, sleep then. (*He gestures toward the bed at frame right.*) Make yourself comfortable and sleep.
MARION (*crossing behind Lucas to the bed*): I do want to go to sleep but at home, at the hotel. I'm going.

She picks up her coat from the bed and begins to put it on.

LUCAS: So you're abandoning the conjugal hovel.
MARION (*laughs, picks up her newspaper, crosses left behind Lucas, and bends over to kiss him*): Good night.
LUCAS: Wait, wait.
MARION: I'm waiting. (*Lucas pulls her head toward him for a much longer kiss.*) I'll come and see you tomorrow morning, as soon as I get in.

Marion exits left as camera pulls in on Lucas, who observes Marion's departure.

240. Backstage. Marc bursts in through the doorway; camera follows him as he moves right toward Bernard, who, in MS range, is seen working on the phonograph he noticed in 220 above.

MARC: Raymond! Raymond! (*to Bernard*) You haven't seen Raymond? I've been looking for him everywhere.
BERNARD: No.
MARC (*to Bernard as he crosses behind him*): Are you the electrician now?
BERNARD: No, not the electrician. The engineer.
MARC (*off-screen*): Raymond! Raymond!

Camera pulls in slowly on the turntable as Bernard adjusts it with a screwdriver.

241. The street alongside the theater. Raymond, carrying a large package rushes toward the stage door and enters.

242. Raymond rushes into the wings; camera pulls back, revealing the whole company assembled. They comment on Raymond's late arrival.

RAYMOND: Yeah, I know, I know. You've been waiting for me. I stood in line for three quarters of an hour at the hardware store. By the time I got out, someone had taken my bicycle. With the chain. So, too bad, I take the subway—and there's a power failure! I'm stuck between two stations.

JEAN-LOUP: You shouldn't have taken the subway. You knew we were in a hurry.

ARLETTE: You should have taken a bicycle-taxi. We would have paid you back.

BERNARD: But they would have charged him double.

ARLETTE: Very funny.

RAYMOND: That's why, that's exactly why I don't take bicycle-taxis. I have some human feelings, you know.

BERNARD: I was only kidding.

RAYMOND (*beginning to cross right, camera following him*): Can you see me spread out like a pasha? Hauled about by some poor bastard sweating blood on his bike? (*There is a general muttering of apologetic comments as the group moves after Raymond.*) Sure, I know. Nice fat men are funny, they make you laugh, they're amusing to have around.

Jean-Loup pats Raymond's face consolingly, but Raymond pushes his hand away.

243. Merlin walks down the steps into the wings, and, framed behind a ladder, peers at the group.

RAYMOND (*off-screen*): It's not easy being a fat man, let me tell you!

244. Resume on backstage group, as at the end of 242.

RAYMOND: And I'm not a nice fat man. I'm a mean fat man. Get off my back!

Raymond turns his back on the others, who mutter "Oh, dear" and "Poor Raymond" and the like. Bernard moves left toward Raymond and touches his shoulder, then continues left across the stage. Jean-Loup and Marc are seen in the background at their table in the orchestra; Marion and Arlette are in the foreground, facing the auditorium.

BERNARD: They stole my bike from me last year, too. So I wrote it off. Three days later, at the other end of Paris—incredible! What do I see? (*He is now addressing his recital principally to Marion and Arlette.*) My bike. Just as I had left it: 813-HK-45. So I say to myself: "But it's my bike, all I have to do is take it."

245. Merlin, as in 243, but now retreating instead of entering.

BERNARD (*off-screen*): Just then some creep walks up, real cool.

246. Resume on Bernard, as at the end of 244.

BERNARD: I let him unlock the chain and then I say "Look, mister, if you don't mind, it's my bike." The guy gets indignant and we start trading insults. At that point, as always happens at times like these, people stop to see what's going on. And what does he have the nerve to do? He starts calling me a fag! (*He turns to Jean-Loup in the orchestra.*) Excuse me, Jean-Loup. (*Jean-Loup waves understandingly.*) And then he says, in front of all those people crowding around, that I had molested him, that I had propositioned him, that kind of stuff. (*He puts his hands to his mouth in mock horror as camera begins to pull in on his face.*) People start giving me looks. They were all on the side of the thief.

247. The cellar. Camera travels down the flue wall to Lucas in MCU, *adjusting a small lamp.*

BERNARD (*off-screen*): I said to myself "That's it. They're going to beat me up." I took off. I'd had enough.

Lucas laughs.

248. The wings. Jacquot sits on a table, clapping his hands each time he remembers another of the words that Raymond is apparently asking him to repeat. Raymond crosses and recrosses in the foreground.

JACQUOT: There are the "boches," [24] the "heinies," the "krauts," the "jerries" . . . I don't remember the others.
RAYMOND: You forgot the "buzzards."
JACQUOT: That's right. The "buzzards."

Bernard enters at frame right, carrying the phonograph; he passes in front of Jacquot and out the door.

BERNARD: Good-bye.
RAYMOND: So long.
JACQUOT: Good-bye.
RAYMOND (*to Bernard, who is framed in the doorway*): Where are you going with my record player?
BERNARD (*stepping forward out of view, then back a step into the door frame*): First of all, it's not your record player, it's Marion's, and she lent it to me for a little party. Good night.

He steps out of view.

RAYMOND: Everything disappears in this theater. (*He crosses right.*) When it's not a rocking chair, it's the record player . . .

249. Outside the stage door. Bernard emerges, carrying the phonograph. He turns right at the corner of the building and walks up the side street, where Christian awaits him. Bernard gives the machine to Christian; Bernard returns toward camera while Christian walks in the other direction for the length of the street to the corner, then turns left out of view.

250. The hotel lobby. Camera focuses on a row of key slots at the desk. Camera pulls back as the clerk removes a key and passes left to hand it to Marion, who is seen from the rear.

DESK CLERK: Madame Steiner, there's a gentleman waiting for you in the bar.
MARION: A gentleman? I've made no appointment.
DESK CLERK: I don't know his name, but it's the gentleman who writes for *Je suis partout.*
MARION (*turning around to look off to her left*): Daxiat.
DESK CLERK: Yes, Daxiat.

Marion exits at frame left.

251. The hotel bar. Daxiat, in MCU, *removes his hat as Marion approaches, then takes a step into two-shot with Marion.*

DAXIAT: I wanted to speak with you for a moment, Madame. I didn't want to see you at the theater. It's confidential. (*He gestures to a nearby table.*) Please sit down. (*Marion crosses in front of Daxiat and seats herself at the table. Camera follows Daxiat as he too seats himself, then holds briefly on him.*) I know you don't like me, but I'm vain enough to think that that's because you don't know me well.

252 to 260. Alternating CUs *of Marion and Daxiat.*

MARION: I'm not judging you. I only know that your articles have often harmed

those I love and whose work I admire. Some say that you really do love the theater. I don't know.

DAXIAT: It's true that I am a walking paradox. I love the theater. I live for the theater. And I'm hated by the vast majority of theater people. Not that I wish to boast, but it takes a certain strength to work in the midst of so much hostility. I think I have this strength. You know that I always admired Lucas Steiner. If he were standing here in front of me right now, I would tell him that our real struggle is a socialist struggle, anticapitalist, and that we too are men of the left. But we want to go further. We want revolution.

MARION: You know, Lucas used to buy all the newspapers, but he would read only the theater page. And I do the same. As for politics . . .

DAXIAT: You're wrong there. Everything is political. In any case, that's your business. That's not why I'm here. (*He removes a document from his pocket.*) Lucas Steiner is still in France.

Daxiat hands the document to Marion, who looks at it and then takes it from him.

261. CU *of an Identification Card. Marion opens it; it bears Lucas's picture and a false name.*

262. CU *of Marion. An air-raid siren is heard on the soundtrack.*

263. CU *of Daxiat. The siren goes on. Daxiat looks upward.*

264. CU *of Marion. She too now looks upward.*

265. LS *of the corner of the bar where Daxiat and Marion are sitting. The desk clerk crosses left, followed by a German officer. The lights dim for a moment.*

DESK CLERK: Ladies and gentlemen, we're sorry. It's idiotic but it can't be helped. Everybody must go to the shelter. To the shelter.

The German officer repeats these instructions in German. Everyone begins to rise. Marion lays the Identification Card on the table; Daxiat reaches for it.

266. The air-raid shelter in the basement of the hotel. A maid carrying a candelabrum is seen walking toward camera past various other hotel employees. In CS *range, she turns right and hands the candelabrum to the clerk, who carries it right, past Marion who, with Daxiat behind her, stands facing the camera in* MC *range.*

DAXIAT (*whispering to Marion*): The Identification Card I showed you was found on a guide who was arrested.
YVONNE (*crossing from frame left*): Good evening, Madame.
MARION: Hello, Yvonne.

Yvonne exits at right foreground.

DAXIAT: Your husband is surely hiding in a small village or in the countryside, but sooner or later he will make contact with you. I'm sure of that.

A German officer crosses left in the foreground. Camera begins to move very slowly in on Marion and Daxiat.

DAXIAT: I have a message I would like you to convey to him. Tell him that if he decides to return to Paris, I will not print anything unfavorable to him in my newspaper. It's a question of honor. (*At this last phrase, Marion half turns toward Daxiat.*) But, if he returns, he will compromise your position. Have you thought of your theater? The name "Steiner" is harmful to you. You should request a divorce.

Marion turns to frame left, away from Daxiat.

267. The cellar. Camera moves left past the table covered with books to the bed, where it follows Lucas's hand as he caresses Marion's legs, then along Lucas's back until Marion is seen in CU *over his left shoulder, her arm around his neck.*

LUCAS: Do you remember, Marion, do you remember?
MARION: What should I remember?
LUCAS: The large elevator on the rue Barbès?
MARION: Yes, yes. I remember. I was sure that everyone knew what we were doing. I was scared to death.
LUCAS (*moving from above Marion to the left of frame beside her, so that their faces are almost touching*): Were you just scared?
MARION: No, not just scared. And what about the time with the designer of the *Doll's House*? That time *you* were scared.[25]
LUCAS: I was very happy. Go on now. Go back to the hotel. I'd rather you left right away.
MARION: How would it be if I stayed here tonight?
LUCAS: All night? Until tomorrow morning?
MARION: All night. Until tomorrow morning.
LUCAS: Really? I'm going to turn off the lights to consider your proposition.

Marion moves to kiss Lucas as he extinguishes the light. The screen goes black.

268. The cellar. Lucas, in CU, *is listening at the hole in the flue wall. He chews vigorously and frowns as he listens.*

BERNARD (*off-screen*): "This is what I came to say. Helena, I love you."

269. On stage. MS *of Bernard and Marion, facing the auditorium as they rehearse.*

BERNARD: "Why do you refuse to listen?"

He gently touches Marion's face with one finger.

MARION (*removing Bernard's hand and turning to face him*): Listen, Bernard. I know a gesture is called for at this point, but I would prefer (*facing front again*) that you didn't touch my face during rehearsal. (*She turns again to Bernard.*) You'll do it during the performance.

270. JEAN-LOUP (*in* MCS, *seated at his table in the orchestra*): Let's pick it up again, kids.

271. Two-shot of Bernard and Marion, closer than 269. Marion's reading of her lines is now especially rapid and detached; at no point does she really look at Bernard.

MARION: "But I don't have the right to love, don't you understand? Neither to love nor to be loved."
BERNARD: "But since I have come to say quite simply 'Helena, I love you,' why do you refuse to listen to me?"

272. JEAN-LOUP (*as in 270*): Bernard, don't forget to touch Marion's face at this point.

273. Resume on Bernard and Marion, as in 271. Bernard looks at Marion, then looks away.

274. Jean-Loup, as in 270.

RAYMOND (*leaning forward, whispering to Jean-Loup*): Marion told him not to touch her.

Jean-Loup leans back and expresses annoyed resignation.

275. In front of the concierge's flat. Camera picks up on Jacquot in the open window, then passes left across the little street and past the corner of the theater to the stage door, from which Merlin, carrying a briefcase, emerges to descend the steps. The shot is accompanied by a radio broadcast.

RADIO ANNOUNCER: This is the scene here; a large crowd is gathered and I'm trying to make my way through with my microphone. (*A loud explosion is heard.*) What's going on? That blast—they say it came from an explosive device in a record player. An assassination attempt! Admiral Fröhlich has been seriously injured! What? They say he's dead. The place is in a panic! They're looking for the terrorists who planted the device. People are running in every direction . . .
A voice from the crowd is heard: Yes, a record player exploded.

276. Documentary ELS *of a metro station.*

277. Marion's offices. Shot begins with a CU *of various jewels, spread out on a black cloth. Camera lifts to show the face of a jeweler, wearing a loupe, who has been examining the gems; at the left is Marion in profile. A knock is heard.*

MERLIN (*off-screen*): Excuse me, Madame Steiner.
MARION: I'm busy, Monsieur Merlin.

278. MERLIN (*at the "Administration" door*): Please. It's important.

279. Resume on Marion and the jeweler. Marion crosses toward the door.

280. Outside the office door. Merlin paces nervously. Marion comes through the doorway and closes the door behind her.

MERLIN: Germaine told me whom you are with. You mustn't sell your jewels at one-fifth of their value. Give them to me. I'll place them with a pawnbroker. And if *The Vanished One* is a hit, in three months you'll be able to redeem them.
MARION (*nodding slightly*): Yes, that's a good idea.

281. Marion and Merlin are seen in silhouette from inside the office.

MARION (*entering and closing the door*): Thank you, Monsieur Merlin. (*She crosses right, to the jeweler, entering* CS *range*.) I'm sorry, but I can't reach a decision today. I have to think over your offer.
JEWELER: As you like, Madame.
MARION: Yes.[26]

282. On stage. Camera follows Arlette as she crosses right, matching a swatch of cloth to a design. She moves toward Bernard, who moves behind her to frame left. In the background, near the apron of the stage, Nadine is heard and seen repeating her lines.

BERNARD: Arlette, won't you come to my dressing room and help me learn my big scene in act two?
ARLETTE (*who had turned to face Bernard and now turns back to the design*): The kind of coaching you want isn't hard to come by. Try a street (*turning contemptuously to Bernard*) where prostitutes hang out.

Arlette turns away and exits at frame right. Bernard mutters "Arlette!" as Nadine comes forward toward him.

NADINE: I can coach you, if you like.
BERNARD: No, thank you, Nadine, I'll manage.
NADINE (*returning to her script and crossing the stage to the right*): "Monsieur Carl, if you want to stay . . . if you want to stay in this house, there is a name you must never utter: the name of Charles-Henri . . ."

Marc is seen casually reading a newspaper at the director's table in the orchestra.

283. The staircase leading to the second floor. Bernard enters, moving quickly up the steps. Camera follows him as he passes Germaine (standing) and Martine (seated) on his way right to the door of his dressing room. Most of Germaine's and Martine's words are spoken out of frame.

MARTINE: Go to the Galeries Lafayette,[27] to the perfume counter, and ask for Mademoiselle Yolande. Use my name. She can get you *Gone with the Wind* for eighty francs.

GERMAINE: I certainly wouldn't pay eighty francs for a book, even on the black market . . .

Bernard opens his dressing-room door, pauses, then turns around and begins to retrace his steps toward Germaine and Martine.

GERMAINE: . . . but if Marion wants it . . .
MARTINE: Yes. She told me she wants to read it.
GERMAINE: I'm off, then.

She begins to exit right as Bernard approaches.

MARTINE: O.K.
BERNARD: Martine, do you want to come to my dressing room with me, to help me learn my lines?
MARTINE: I don't know. I never did that.
BERNARD: It's very simple. (*He tries to rid her of the large case lying on her lap. She holds on to the case, rises, then places the case on the chair.*) All you do is read. I read a line and you answer me.
MARTINE: Fine. O.K.
BERNARD: Let's go.
MARTINE (*to Germaine*): Will you watch my box?
GERMAINE: Sure.

Bernard and Martine exit frame left as Germaine reenters and watches them with a knowing smile as they close the dressing room door behind them.

MARTINE (*off-screen*): It's nice in here.
BERNARD: Yes. It's my dressing room.

284. The cellar. Lucas, in his black hat, sits behind his writing table, staring at the radio at the left of frame.

RADIO ANNOUNCER: They came above all to make a profit, not really to work. The problem stems from the fact that most Frenchmen are not capable of recognizing a Jew.

Lucas faces forward. As he hears Marion descending the spiral staircase, he turns to her, motions her to be silent, points to the radio, then faces front again. Marion has moved to a place just behind Lucas.

RADIO ANNOUNCER: If they could, they would be on their guard. But they can't. There are those whose faces are clearly Jewish. But not all. The problem wouldn't arise if, for example, Jews had blue skin. But this is not the case. We must therefore be able to recognize them. That is why—

Lucas snaps off the radio. Marion has placed her hands on his shoulders.

LUCAS: They say that it's better to hear this stuff than to be deaf. But sometimes I wonder whether it wouldn't be better to be deaf.
MARION (*removing Lucas's hat and bending over to place her face against his*): Did you listen to the last rehearsal?
LUCAS: Yes, it was terrific. (*Marion straightens up and crosses right.*) That is, incomparably better. When it is whispered, the scene plays very well. (*Lucas gestures with his folded eyeglasses as camera moves in on him.*) But in order to preserve the sense of intimacy, the lighting should create the same effect. The faces should be lit from behind. Like silhouettes.

285. On stage. The set has almost completely taken shape. In a large bay window of the set, center, stand Marion and Bernard in LS range. In the foreground, seated on the stage, sits Jean-Loup.

JEAN-LOUP: Don't move, kids. You're silhouettes. (*Raymond enters the rear of the set from the right.*) Please, Raymond, we're working.

Raymond rushes off to the left.

ARLETTE (*entering the set from the left*): What a wonderful idea, Jean-Loup. I'll shift the backdrop so that the silhouettes are even sharper. That will work very well.

The screen suddenly goes dark.

JEAN-LOUP: Damn it, Raymond, what are you doing? The lights have gone out!

Various characters enter the darkened stage, carrying lit kerosene lamps and candles. Dimly seen, they move about in confusion.

RAYMOND: I know the lights are out. I know. It's not me. It's the whole neighborhood.
NADINE: It's a power failure.
BERNARD: Perfect for silhouettes!
GERMAINE: I looked out the window and the whole neighborhood is dark. You'd think they'd warn us.
RAYMOND: Marc, come with me, let's go find what we need to get some light.
MARC: O.K.
GERMAINE: I know where there are candles. For a price, naturally.

286. The stairway to the second floor. In near darkness, Marion ascends, carrying a lighted lantern. Camera follows as she turns the corner toward a door marked "Nadine Marsac."

287. Marion opens the door without knocking. Framed in the doorway are Nadine and Arlette, passionately embracing. Marion at once closes the door, pauses for an instant, and, again without knocking, opens the door—as if the first interruption had not taken place.

288. Nadine's dressing room. As the door opens, Nadine and Arlette stand facing Marion in MS range; Nadine is buttoning her blouse.

MARION (*in the foreground, off-screen*): Nadine, we're waiting for you to rehearse downstairs.

Nadine and Arlette turn to face each other.

289. Resume on Marion, as at the end of 287. Closing the door, she walks toward camera. Arlette follows as Marion comes to the end of the corridor and turns left.

ARLETTE: Marion, I'd like to explain.
MARION: There's nothing to explain.

The two now stand in MS *range before the "Administration" door.*

ARLETTE: Don't judge me too harshly.
MARION: I'm not judging you. I would simply prefer that you conduct your love life outside the theater.

Marion opens the door and enters; her lantern creates a bright circle of light from inside the door before it disappears at the left. Arlette begins to exit at the right.

290. On the darkened stage. Raymond stands holding a lamp.

ARLETTE (*off-screen, sobbing*): Marion has no pity. She's heartless. She's too cold.

Bernard enters through the doorway to Raymond's left. He pauses and turns his head to look left, in the direction of Arlette.

ARLETTE (*off-screen*): She doesn't care about anyone.

Camera moves left to Arlette and Jean-Loup, lit by the lamp Jean-Loup is holding.

ARLETTE (*leaning against him, from time to time hiding her face on his shoulder, and continuing to sob*): She never forgives anyone anything. She never even looked at me. She's even worse since Lucas went away. I can't stand it any more. I've had enough.

Holding Arlette, Jean-Loup proceeds to guide her to the left as camera follows. She continues to sob and wipe her tears.

JEAN-LOUP: Calm yourself. Calm yourself, old girl. It's not the end of the world. What happened? Marion pushed open a door that should have been locked from the inside. Right now, it seems like a big tragedy. Two weeks from now, no one will even remember that it happened. You know that's true.
ARLETTE: If only it were. In any case, I can't stay. I want to go home.

JEAN-LOUP: Run along.
ARLETTE: Bye bye. You're a dear.

They arrive at the exit. Arlette steps into the doorway. Jean-Loup follows her and kisses her cheek. Still sobbing, Arlette exits.

BERNARD (*entering at frame left and moving toward Jean-Loup*): Should I take her home?
JEAN-LOUP (*emerging from the doorway and moving with Bernard toward camera*): No, forget it, forget it. That's exactly what you mustn't do. On the contrary. Things must right themselves. Forget it.
BERNARD: But she's so unhappy, so upset. (*He pauses and seats himself.*) Christ, I really was on the wrong track with that woman.
JEAN-LOUP: That's for sure. Arlette is no partner for you—she's more like a competitor. (*He pauses.*) You really liked her that much?
BERNARD (*rising and stepping toward the doorway, then back again*): I just wanted to go to bed with her. I don't know why. It was like wanting a warm croissant.
JEAN-LOUP (*taking Bernard's arm and guiding him left out of frame*): A few times I wanted to warn you that you were making a mistake, but then . . . I thought I should mind my own business.

291. The cellar. Lucas, bespectacled, lies sprawled casually on the bed, cutting the pages of a book. He glances occasionally to the left; camera follows as he rises and crosses to Marion, who is setting the table. He seats himself.

LUCAS: So, you're going to spend the evening at La Joconde. But La Joconde is a nightclub. You know what they say on London radio. They say that those who spend their evenings in nightclubs will have to explain themselves after the war. Yes, they do.
MARION: Oh, it's Jean-Loup's idea. He thinks it will be good for our morale. (*She crosses left and stirs the pot on the gas burner.*) When you were running the theater, you had a right to your moods. Sometimes you would take us out partying. Sometimes you would retire to your room. But when it comes to me, I'm not sure why, I have to be there all the time, the charming manager, always smiling. (*She lifts the pot off the burner and begins to cross right.*) Even Jean-Loup complains about me.

Marion crosses behind Lucas and begins to ladle soup into his bowl.

LUCAS: Jean-Loup is right. And he doesn't know the whole of it. That you neglect me, well, we'll let that pass. I've come to terms with that. But for the others up there, the play comes before anything else. You need to look after them more. (*Marion places her hand on the back of Lucas's chair. Lucas looks up to her.*) Why don't you answer me?

MARION: If I answered you, I might be too cruel. Everything is ready. The coffee is there. I'm going.

Lucas begins to eat his soup as Marion exits at frame right.

292. Marion is seen from the rear walking toward the spiral staircase, which she begins to ascend.

LUCAS (*off-screen*): Marion?
MARION: Yes.

293. LUCAS (*in* MCU *at the table*): I heard the love scene between you and Bernard through the vent.

MARION (*off-screen*): Yes? And so?
LUCAS: I don't know, it seemed to me . . .

294. Marion is seen in MCU *through the railing of the staircase.*

LUCAS (*off-screen*): It could have been better.
MARION: What exactly are you trying to tell me?

295. LUCAS (*in* CU, *looking at Marion*): It's the only love scene in the play . . .

296. Marion, in the same position on the staircase but now in CU.

LUCAS (*off-screen*): Try to play it with more sincerity.

Marion lowers her eyes, nods very slightly, glances back at Lucas, and continues to climb the stairs.

297. At the nightclub. The singer stands on stage, a microphone before her and a few musicians behind her. She puffs on her cigarette holder, then begins to

*sing. Camera moves across a room filled with attentive listeners (among them
many German officers) seated at tables. Camera finally settles on the hat-check
booth, behind which a young Oriental woman takes a German officer's cap.
Also standing before the booth is Nadine, who turns and walks toward camera,
looking in both directions as if searching for someone. Finally camera follows
as she crosses right, past several tables, to a table in the right corner of the
room. At this table are seated Marion, Jean-Loup, and Arlette. Moving past
Arlette, Nadine squeezes her uplifted hand, then kisses Jean-Loup on the cheek.
Nadine moves in as if to seat herself between Marion and Jean-Loup.*

NADINE: Good evening.
MARION: Good evening.
NADINE: How's everything?
MARION: No, Nadine. That's Bernard's place.

The song that accompanies this shot and the following shots begins as follows:

> Since, one night, in a corner of France,
> I saw your immense eyes in the shadows,
> My heart has been full of mad hope.
> I think of you day and night.

> But our languages aren't the same,
> And in order to say that I love you
> I know no poem lovelier
> Than these tender words from my homeland:
> "Bei mir bist du schön . . ."[28]

298 to 302. Alternating CUs *of Nadine and Marion.*

NADINE: Oh. In any case, I can't stay. I came to ask you to excuse me. I have
  an appointment with the producer of *Angels of Mercy*. I'm not sure it's going
  to work. There are two other girls who are up for the part. They wouldn't
  say who.
MARION: It's a wonderful part. I'd be very happy for you if you got it.
JEAN-LOUP (*off-screen*): We'll keep our fingers crossed, Nadine dear.

NADINE: I'm off. Good night.
MARION: Good night.

303. CU of Marion, who watches Nadine as she crosses in front of camera and exits left. Marion then looks still farther left, presumably at the hat-check booth.

304. MS of the Oriental woman behind the hat-check counter.

305. MLS of singer:

> I'd have preferred, all the same.
> To tell you everything in French.
> My heart is beating . . .

306 to 310. Alternating CUs of Marion and CU two-shots of Jean-Loup and Arlette.

ARLETTE: I'm sure she'll give a good reading, but I don't think she'll get the part. Nadine is still a baby. She would do better in *School for Wives*.[29]
JEAN-LOUP: *School for Wives*? Nadine in the role of Agnès? It's fine with me, but when she says "The little cat is dead," I suspect that everyone in the audience will think she did it.

Everyone laughs.

311. BERNARD (*entering left in* MC *range*): Everyone seems to be having a good time here.

312. MARION (*in* CU): There you are, Bernard. Come sit next to me.

BERNARD (*off-screen*): Sure, but I'm not alone. I came with a friend.

313. BERNARD (*leading a young woman into frame*): Simone. Take care of her for a minute. I'm going to put all this in the checkroom and I'll be right back.

314. CU *of Marion, who watches Bernard leave.*

SIMONE (*off-screen*): Good evening.
MARION (*sipping her wine and signaling to Arlette with her eyes*): Arlette, will you sit next to me?

315. At the hat-check booth. Bernard hands his coat and hat to the Oriental woman, who asks him to wait for his ticket. As Bernard waits, he looks at the shelves behind the counter.

316. Camera moves along the seemingly endless collection of German military caps on the shelves.

317. BERNARD (CU): Wait, excuse me, Mademoiselle, give me back my things. I've changed my mind.

318. The Oriental woman returns Bernard's things. As Bernard exits frame to the right, his place at the counter is taken by Daxiat, who glances after Bernard and then moves in the opposite direction.

319. The corner table in MS *range.*

BERNARD (*entering from the left*): I'm terribly sorry, Madame Steiner, I can't stay. (*to Simone*) Come, we're going. I had completely forgotten an appointment.
MARION: You're free, Bernard, everyone is free.

Simone rises to leave with Bernard.

BERNARD: So please excuse me, everyone. See you tomorrow. Good-bye.
ARLETTE: Good-bye.

320. MCU *of the singer:*

"Bei mir bist du schön,"
That means in the language of love,
"Darling, I'm yours forever."

321. CU *of Marion, sipping her wine.*

322. ELS *of other tables in the nightclub.*

323. MCS *of Bernardini, shifting about in his seat to stare at Marion's table.*

324. Marion, Arlette, and Jean-Loup at their table.

ARLETTE: There's a man over there who has been staring at us. Don't look now, but he's coming over.

Jean-Loup turns and rises.

BERNARDINI (*entering from the right and shaking Jean-Loup's hand*): Hello there, Cottins. Everything going well?

325. MC *shot of Marion and Arlette, who both turn away from Bernardini.*

BERNARDINI (*off-screen*): Are you still in show business?
JEAN-LOUP (*off-screen*): Naturally. I'm a trouper.
BERNARDINI (*off-screen*): Say, Cottins, will you introduce me?
JEAN-LOUP (*off-screen*): I'm terribly sorry, I've forgotten your first name.

326. CU *of Jean-Loup and Bernardini.*

BERNARDINI: René. René Bernardini.
JEAN-LOUP: Yes, yes, of course. René Bernardini, Arlette Guillaume, Marion Steiner.

Bernardini bows to Marion.

327. Marion and Arlette, as in 325. Marion extends her hand to Bernardini, who kisses it.

MARION: Good evening.
ARLETTE: Excuse me, Marion, I'll be back in a minute.
MARION: You're coming back, aren't you?
ARLETTE: Yes, yes. Excuse me.

She rises, leaves the table, and begins to cross left.

328. Arlette crosses the room to the left.

329. MLS *of the singer, now finishing her number:* "Tell me that you love me." *She acknowledges the audience's applause.*

330. The corner table. Bernardini now sits in Arlette's place.

BERNARDINI (*sipping his wine*): I don't know about you, but I don't think it's much fun here. (*He turns to Marion.*) Let's all go to the Monseigneur.
JEAN-LOUP: No, no, no, no. Marion is very tired because we are in the midst of rehearsals.
MARION: Listen, Jean-Loup, stop making decisions for me. I feel like going to the Monseigneur.
JEAN-LOUP: But Marion, let's at least wait for Arlette.
MARION: No, no, no, no, no. You're both killjoys. I'm not sleepy. It's really spooky in here. (*She reaches for Bernardini's hand.*) Shall we go?

Camera follows as Marion and Bernardini leave the table and cross left.

ARLETTE (*meeting them on her way back to the table*): What's going on here?
MARION: Good-bye. I'm on my own.

Arlette watches them leave, then returns to the table and sits beside Jean-Loup.

ARLETTE: What's going on here?
JEAN-LOUP: That's just like Marion. She sees that the evening is spoiled, so she'll spoil it all the way.

331. Marion's hotel room. Camera picks up on the door. Yvonne enters carrying a tray. She looks toward the bed. Swish pan to the bed: it has clearly not been slept in.

332. MCU *of Yvonne. She turns and exits, closing the door behind her.*

333. CU *of the seating model of the theater, now placed on the stage. Arlette, standing on the floor of the orchestra, points to it. Marion and Jean-Loup stand on the stage on either side of it.*

ARLETTE: I see where Daxiat will be sitting. He has numbers 17 and 19, middle of the seventh row.

334. Reverse of 333: the model is now in the foreground, seen from the rear. In addition to Marion, Jean-Loup, and Arlette, shot reveals Marc, Bernard, Raymond, and Merlin sitting in the background in the orchestra.

JEAN-LOUP: Don't forget the twenty seats for the Propaganda Bureau, either. (*The men in the background laugh.*) What are you laughing about? It's required. Twenty seats each night. I didn't make up the rule.

335. Closer shot of Bernard, Raymond, and Merlin in the orchestra.

MERLIN: At the Théâtre de l'Odeon, they give them the side boxes, so if they don't fill the boxes it's not serious.

336. Jean-Loup and Marion, facing the seating model.

MARION: We'll do as they do at the Odéon. We'll place them in the side boxes.

337. A corridor on the second floor of the theater. As the discussion of the seating plan continues, barely audible on the soundtrack, Martine moves stealthily toward camera, checking doors as she passes them; at one door she knocks, opens, peers inside, and enters.

338. Marion, Arlette, and Jean-Loup, as in 334.

ARLETTE: That's really too much. We give the best seats to people who take pleasure in panning us and we refuse four seats to people who are enthusiastic from the beginning.
JEAN-LOUP: But you know what Lucas would have said? "Give the best seats to your enemies."

339. On stage.

NADINE (*entering left foreground in* CU *range*): Excuse me, Marion. Germaine, did you arrange things in my dressing room? I can't find my pocketbook.

340. Resume on 338. Everyone rises to follow Nadine off to the left.

341. All those assembled in the theater pass from the wings to the back stairway.

342. The second floor. The shot opens on Bernard, seen through a doorway, as he goes through a desk drawer. Camera follows the several members of the company who cross and recross, pass along hallways, in and out of doorways, etc., all the while discussing the theft.

GERMAINE (*off-screen*): My goodness, what a mess! Someone was in here poking around.
BERNARD: I can't find my little traveling clock, but I don't know—I don't think anything else is missing.
GERMAINE: My word, it's like a den of thieves.
MARION: How about you, Jean-Loup? What's missing?
JEAN-LOUP: I found my wallet, but it's empty.
MARION: So it's most serious for you, Nadine.
NADINE: Yes. The money, well, I don't mind that so much. But I've lost my food rations, my Identification Card, my work permit, and above all my pass to go out at night.
ARLETTE: It's a good thing I locked your dressing room, Marion.
MARC: Do you want me to call the police, Madame Steiner?
MARION: Absolutely not. We'll do our own investigating.
JEAN-LOUP: Here's what they reported on Radio Paris last week. Some moving men came by to pick up a piano. And the piano was never seen again.

Shot ends with Jean-Loup and Nadine in MS *range.*

JEAN-LOUP: Those moving men were no more moving men than I am.
NADINE: That's a good story, but it doesn't get me my papers back. In any case, I'd really like to know who did it.

343. On stage. Shot opens with CU *of Germaine; camera pulls back to reveal Bernard, Marion, and Arlette grouped around her.*

GERMAINE: I know who did it. I'm pretty sure, at least. Excuse me, Raymond. You know who I'm thinking of. I'm sure you won't agree with me.

344. RAYMOND (*in the orchestra, rising and crossing left*): But yes, I do agree. Of course, naturally, it was her. I had that figured out right away.

345. Resume on Bernard, Germaine, Marion, and Arlette as in 343.

GERMAINE: Only Martine could have done it. She's the only one who—
MARION (*interrupting*): Look, Raymond. We're not going to get the police mixed up in this. You go right to Martine's house and try to—
BERNARD (*interrupting*): If you'd rather, Raymond, I'll go with you.
RAYMOND (*off-screen*): But I don't know where she lives!
GERMAINE: But after all, she is your woman.

346. RAYMOND (*as at the end of 344*): No, she's not. She wouldn't. She goes from theater to theater to sell her black-market stuff and that's how I met her. Once I took her to the movies, another time to a restaurant. But that's all. I swear. I don't know her address.

347. CU *of Marion, who lowers her eyes; Bernard and Arlette stand on either side just behind her.*

RAYMOND (*off-screen*): I've never been to her house . . .

348. Resume on Raymond.

RAYMOND: . . . and she never came to mine. Only, since she's a pretty girl, I liked the idea that everyone thought we were sleeping together.

349. Resume on Marion, as in 347. Bernard, at left, smiles and looks away.

MERLIN (*off-screen*): Madame Steiner, in that case, we should call the police.
NADINE (*barely visible at frame left*): Yes, the police.

MARION: I guess I didn't make myself clear. I don't want the police to set foot in this theater.

350. Outside the theater, near the box office. Raymond crosses back and forth, directing the queue waiting for tickets.

RAYMOND: Please, ladies, please, form a straight line. Leave the passage open. Thank you, thank you.

Marion walks from the street toward camera. She comes up the theater steps.

FEMALE VOICE (*off-screen*): Are there any seats for this evening's performance?
RAYMOND: No, Madame, tonight's by invitation only. It's opening night. Good evening, Madame Steiner.
MARION: Good evening.

Camera follows Marion as she crosses right past the queue, then holds on two women near the box-office window, one of whom says "Did you see that woman? It's Marion Steiner."

351. The stairway leading to the second floor. Arlette enters at the top frame left, a boy carrying a large basket of flowers at the bottom from frame right. They cross on the stairs.

BOY: They told me to take these to the manager's office, but I don't know where it is.
ARLETTE: It's the glass door on the landing.

Camera follows the boy to the top of the stairs. Next to the "Administration" door, in MS range, stands Nadine in her maid's costume.

NADINE: Are you looking for Madame Steiner? Her dressing room is over there.
GERMAINE (*opening the door from the inside*): No, no, no. Put them in the office. If Marion wants to rest, I don't want her to be poisoned.

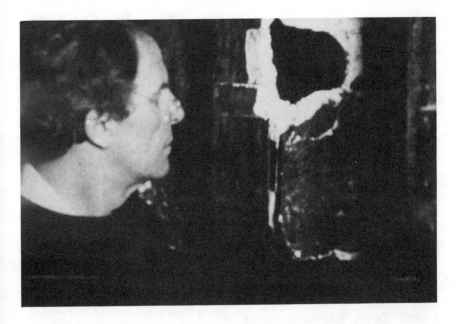

Nadine crosses to the right of the door. From frame right appears Marc in his gamekeeper's costume; camera follows him as he crosses left, muttering his lines, then as he moves around a pillar, then as he crosses right toward Nadine, who smiles and gives him a small flower.

352. The cellar. Lucas in his black hat is seen in profile in MS *range, listening at the hole in the wall of the flue.*

LUCAS: I can hear them, Marion. I can hear them. (*He turns to face camera, which retreats as he walks toward it. Camera then follows Lucas as he turns left and crosses the cellar apartment to the table, where Marion is seated, eating.*) Do you hear them? I don't know how you can eat. I couldn't.
MARION (*holding a piece of bread up to Lucas*): Sure you can. Here.
LUCAS: No, I assure you, I can't. I can only think of one thing: what's going to happen if it's a disaster tonight?

MARION: We'll put on another play.

LUCAS (*starting to cross left behind Marion*): With what money? Tell me that. With what money? Have you seen the accounts? I've looked at them. If *The Vanished One* falls flat, we'll lose the theater. (*He is now at the left of the table. He gestures at Marion and walks forward, out of view.*) It's frightening and I don't understand how you can be so calm.

MARION (*still eating*): Listen, Lucas. You chose the play. You decided on the staging. We followed your directions. It's your effort the audience will see tonight. If it doesn't work . . .

LUCAS (*reentering at left foreground and crossing back to the right of the table, then sitting*): If it doesn't work, if it doesn't work, it will be my fault, my fault alone, my most grievous fault. That won't keep it from being a pile of shit.

MARION (*extending a glass to Lucas*): Here. Drink.

LUCAS: I just don't know how you do it. I can hardly stand on my feet. (*He burps.*) I'm sick to my stomach.

He lays his hand across his stomach.

MARION (*rising*): Listen, calm down.

Lucas rises and walks toward camera; Marion steps back to get a blanket, then follows Lucas as he moves toward the rocking chair.

MARION: Here. I'll get a blanket to put over your lap. Sit down.

Lucas sits. Marion places a blanket across his lap.

LUCAS: Thank you.

MARION (*kneeling*): There. (*A bell begins to ring insistently.*) I have to go. You'll listen closely. Later you'll tell me what you think, right?

LUCAS: Yes.

MARION (*rising and moving toward camera*): I'll see you soon.

LUCAS (*as Marion disappears past camera*): I should be the one to reassure you.

MARION (*off-screen*): I don't need to be reassured. I feel light as a feather.

Her footsteps are heard on the staircase.

353. The staircase to the second floor. Marion rushes up the stairs, around a corner, and toward a door marked "Toilettes," which she opens. Through the open doorway, we see that she is throwing up into the toilet bowl just out of view at the left of the door frame.

354. E L S of the orchestra, now filled.

355. E L S of the stage, the curtain closed.

356. The wings. Marion enters CU range, turns her head toward camera, closes her eyes, and breathes deeply. She then opens her eyes and turns away. Camera follows as she moves onto the stage and up the step to the landing that leads to the steps of the set. In profile, she looks right.

357. E L S of the orchestra, panning slightly. On the soundtrack come the three pounding noises that customarily announce the beginning of a performance.

358 to 362. Series of very brief shots of Raymond pounding the club, of Lucas listening at his hole, of Raymond again, of the audience with a handsome German soldier in center frame, and of Rosette seated in the audience.

N A D I N E (*off-screen*): "Isn't Master Eric with you, Madame?"

363. The stage. Now in full view is Arlette's extraordinary set. Basically a "realistic" Ibsenesque design, it differs from most examples of the genre by the severity of its lines, its almost total lack of curved corners, the extreme spareness of its furnishings, and its muted but striking color scheme of peach, salmon, and pink. Marion and Nadine, carrying a tray, face each other.

M A R I O N: "He couldn't sit still this morning. But I think I know where he is. He must be at the front gate keeping watch on the road."

364. Another E L S of the audience. Though Rosette is still visible, from this angle hers is only one of many attentive faces.

N A D I N E (*off-screen*): "Master Eric begged to go to the station, but Doctor Sanders would not allow it."

365. Marion and Nadine, now in MS *range.*

MARION: "My godfather always knows what is best. I suppose he wanted to
   be alone with the tutor to speak about his new student. Naturally, if Doctor
   Sanders had asked my opinion, I would have told him that Eric doesn't need
   a tutor. He is still . . ."

366. CU *of Lucas, sitting beside his hole and listening, mouthing the lines as
he hears them.*

MARION (*off-screen*): ". . . so young, and it gives me so much pleasure to
   teach him the little I know."

367. Resume on Marion and Nadine.

NADINE: "You are right, Madame. I think, however, that this big house is too
   quiet for Master Eric." (*She turns and moves right as camera follows.*) "You
   know, my mother told me that when she was working at the estate there were
   as many as twenty people for dinner."

*368. The wings. Raymond stands beside a man wearing a fire helmet; he also
wears a yellow Star of David. Pointing to his star and turning to Raymond,*

THE MAN: There are twenty-five of us in Paris. We are essential to the public
   welfare.

*369. On stage. Marion and Nadine are now seen from a new angle, with Marion
in the foreground and Nadine upstage. At the edge of the set, Jean-Loup is
visible in the wings.*

MARION: "And on my birthday, when Doctor Sanders told me that from that
   day forward I would eat with the grown-ups, I couldn't keep from crying."

*370. The lobby. Merlin greets the concierge, whom he helps to pass through
the crowd, which includes photographers.*

MAN IN CROWD: Why does that woman get to go in?

JACQUOT'S MOTHER: I have a son who's in the cast. I'm his mother.
That's why.

*371. The wings. Bernard enters from the landing, moving toward camera. As
he proceeds, he pauses to talk to Raymond, then ducks beneath a backdrop
support and moves to a stage entrance where, in* MS *range, he awaits his cue.*

RAYMOND: How are you doing? (*Bernard makes a gesture of total helpless-
ness.*) You know what the boss used to say about the theater, my boy:
"When you have to go, you have to go."

Meanwhile, the play continues.

NADINE (*off-screen*): "May I leave you, Madame? I should prepare the
room."
JEAN-LOUP (*off-screen*): "Tell Eric to finish his lessons before the new tutor
arrives. Helena . . ."

*372. On stage. Now, from a more distant and higher angle, we see Marion and
Jean-Loup playing their scene. Bernard enters from the doorway near the right
of the set. As Marion sees him, she utters a little scream and recoils; Jean-
Loup moves to greet Bernard.*

JEAN-LOUP: ". . . I would like to introduce Monsieur Carl, the new tutor.
Yes, please forgive me, I should have warned you."

373. ELS *of the audience, watching intently.*

JEAN-LOUP (*off-screen*): "The resemblance is extraordinary . . ."

374. On stage. MCU *of Jacquot, in character, seating at a writing desk. He
looks up in surprise.*

JEAN-LOUP (*off-screen*): ". . . absolutely extraordinary."

375. On stage.

MARION (*in* MLS, *keeping her eyes averted from Bernard's*): "I don't know what resemblance you mean." (*She turns toward Jean-Loup and Bernard.*) "We hadn't considered a student, but a man of some experience."

376. MS *of Jean-Loup and Bernard. Camera follows as Bernard crosses the stage to Marion.*

BERNARD: "But Madame, I can show you letters of recommendation."
MARION (*moving right*): "I am not questioning your knowledge."

377. The rear of the orchestra. There is some confusion, and some shushing from the audience, as Daxiat makes his late entrance.

MARION (*off-screen*): "What I am saying is that for this child, who has been raised solely by his uncle and by myself, we felt it best that he be guided by someone . . . I don't know. You are here now. I will leave it to my godfather's judgment."

378. On stage. Jacquot enters frame to stand between Marion and Jean-Loup in MLS *range. Marion places her hand on Jacquot's shoulder and directs him right, toward Bernard.*

MARION: "Eric, please greet your new tutor."

379. The orchestra. Daxiat creates a further disturbance as he seeks to enter his row.

JEAN-LOUP (*off-screen*): "Be calm, Helena. Your memory has no doubt failed you."

380. On stage. Bernard stands with his hand on Jacquot's shoulder. Bernard glances at the orchestra.

JEAN-LOUP (*off-screen*): "This is Monsieur Carl's letter of application . . ."

381. On stage, CU *of Marion and Jean-Loup.*

JEAN-LOUP: "... and I can assure you that you read it only a month ago."

MARION (*taking the letter and glancing over it at the orchestra, then raising the letter to hide her face and whispering to Jean-Loup*): What a creep your friend Daxiat is. (*She steps back into character.*) "Yes, uncle. You are right."

382. The orchestra. Daxiat settles himself into his seat and crosses his arms, watching the stage attentively.

MARION (*off-screen*): "I was confused."

JEAN-LOUP (*off-screen*): "By the resemblance, no doubt."

MARION (*off-screen*): "I don't know. Every new face upsets me. I takes me a few days to get used to things."

383. On stage. Jacquot and Bernard, in MLS range, watch Marion.

MARION (*off-screen*): "And Eric seems very happy."

JACQUOT: "Mother, may I show Monsieur Carl around the estate?"

Bernard turns to look at Jacquot, then back to Marion.

JEAN-LOUP (*off-screen*): "Yes, yes. You may go, my child."

Bernard and Jacquot exit. Bernard steals another glance at the orchestra.

384. The cellar. Camera travels down past the hole in the flue wall to show a bespectacled Lucas, in CS range, briskly taking notes at his table. The ashtray is full.

MARION (*off-screen*): "Listen to me, Gregory."

JEAN-LOUP (*off-screen*): "Helena, my dear Helena. When will you learn to trust me? Don't you know that I'm the one who loves you best? And besides, there's one other thing."

385. Lucas, in profile, drawing on the end of a cigarette.

MARION (*off-screen*): "What is it?"

JEAN-LOUP (*off-screen*): "I cannot lose you."

Lucas listens and looks upward as the audience bursts into applause.

ELS *of audience applauding.*

386. Marion's dressing room. Marion rushes in from the foreground, removing her costume. In MLS *range, she hands it to Germaine.*

MARION: Let's go, Germaine. (*As Marion begins to remove her shift, Germaine turns to face right.*) Germaine!

Camera follows as Germaine hurries to the right. Coming to Jacquot, she sets him firmly with his face against the door.

MARION (*off-screen*): We only have five minutes!
GERMAINE (*to Jacquot*): Don't move. Stay there. (*She rushes back left out of frame as camera holds on Jacquot.*)
GERMAINE (*off-screen*): So, it's going well. You are happy with it?
MARION (*off-screen*): I don't know. I don't want to say anything until it's all over.

387. On stage. Extreme high angle shot of Raymond directing the changing of the flats. He mutters phrases like "Take her up!" and "Easy!"

388. ELS *of the audience awaiting the next act. The house lights dim.*

389. Backstage. Marc in his gamekeeper's costume descends the stairs.

390. In front of the box office (over which a large photo of Lucas is now plainly seen), Merlin tries to placate the crowd.

MAN IN CROWD: What's going on? It's ten minutes past eleven.
MERLIN: That's right. We lost five minutes at intermission.
VOICES FROM CROWD: Can't you let us in? *and* We won't make any noise, of course.

391. MCU *of Daxiat in his seat. The performance has resumed.*

BERNARD (*off-screen*): "I want to tell you something about Doctor Sanders."

392. On stage. Bernard, holding a lantern, and Marion, in a tattered dress, stand in the large bay window.

MARION (*recoiling*): "No. Be quiet. You have no right."
BERNARD: "I'm going to speak, Helena. I must."
MARION: "No!"
BERNARD: "I have proof that Doctor Sanders came back not the day after but the day before the death of Charles-Henri."

Marion cries out and swoons onto the window seat. A gasp rises from the audience. The stage lights go out.

393. ELS *of rapt audience.*

394. Backstage. A brief cut to the man with the fire helmet and Star of David.

395. On stage. In near darkness, Bernard helps Marion up from the floor. Two stagehands hurry by. The stage lights go up again. The stagehands pick up a rug from the stage floor, then exit left past the helmeted man, who continues to listen. Camera moves right to pick up on Germaine, who knits as she listens.

BERNARD (*off-screen*): "Since I have come into this house, I've heard nothing but lies. And these lies contradict each other terribly."

396. On stage. Marion reclines on a couch as Bernard stands beside her.

MARION: "They were not lies. They were lapses in memory. For years, I was the first to seek the truth. Don't you understand how terrible it is not to know who I was, what I did? And still worse, to live in fear that it might happen again? At times I had the impression that I really didn't exist."
BERNARD (*taking hold of her*): "But since I came to tell you very simply: 'Helena, I love you,' why did you refuse to listen to me?"

397. The audience; the focus now is on Bernardini.

398. On stage. The point of view now is that of the balcony audience.

MARION: "I didn't have the right to love. Do you understand that? I didn't have the right to love, nor to be loved."

She crosses downstage. Bernard follows her.

BERNARD: "And now?"

399. Bernard and Marion in MLS *face front. The perspective is once more eye-level.*

MARION: "Now I come to love, Carl, and it is painful. Does love hurt?"
BERNARD: "Yes, love hurts." (*He turns and walks a few steps away from Marion.*) "Like great birds of prey it glides above us. It stops and threatens us. But this threat may also be the promise of happiness." (*He steps back to Marion.*) "You are beautiful, Helena, so beautiful that to look at you is painful."
MARION: "Yesterday you said it was a joy."
BERNARD: "It is a joy. And a torment."

400. Once again seen from the point of view of the balcony, Bernard places his hands on Marion's shoulders; the curtains close, and applause breaks out. The curtains reopen, and Bernard and Marion bow.

401. CU *of Rosette in the audience, applauding.*

402. CU *of Bernardini in the audience, applauding.*

403. CU *of script pages being assembled by Lucas.*

404. Marion and Bernard, seen from the rear, face the audience and accept its applause. The curtains close. Marion and Bernard turn to each other.

MARION (*grinning*): We brought it off!

Marion kisses a surprised Bernard on the lips, then gestures and calls to the other members of the cast to join them for curtain calls. The curtains reopen, and the cast steps to the footlights to bow.

405 to 409. Various shots of the cast bowing, intercut with shots of Daxiat, who applauds, rises from his seat, continues to applaud, smiles, and finally turns to leave as the general applause dies down.

410. JEAN-LOUP (*at the entrance to the backstage area, keeping the crowds back*): No, I'm terribly sorry, my friends. Excuse me, but very frankly, Marion is exhausted. It's a terribly trying role. She needs to rest. (*Arlette passes through the crowd, excusing herself.*) Yes, come on through—it went well, didn't it? (*He returns to the crowd.*) Drop her a line instead. That will please her ever so much more. (*A blonde Frenchwoman pushes her way through the crowd with her husband, a German officer.*) Ah, you came. I didn't know you were here. (*He returns to the crowd.*) Good evening.

411. On stage, where a party is in progress. Camera follows Raymond and Marc as they enter with champagne and glasses.

MARION: You can put them there.

Camera now stays with Marion as she moves right and pauses to exchange comments and congratulations with Nadine and Arlette.

412. MS *of Bernard, watching.*

413. Resume on Marion, Nadine, and Arlette, as at the end of 411, chatting. Jean-Loup takes Marion's arm and leads her right to the blonde Frenchwoman and her husband. The husband kisses Marion's hand and apologizes in German for his inability to speak French.

414. Resume on Bernard, as in 412.

415. Marion, facing the blonde woman and her husband, as at the end of 413.

FRENCHWOMAN: My husband is so sorry that he cannot speak French.

The husband now compliments Marion in German.

416. Resume on Bernard, as in 412.

RAYMOND (*entering at the left and offering him some champagne*): Why the long face? Why do you look so sad?
BERNARD: I'm not sad. (*He touches glasses with Raymond.*) Cheers. It went well.

417. Resume on Marion, who passes right to greet and chat with other well-wishers.

418. Resume on Bernard, again watching Marion.

419. Resume on Marion, chatting with two guests. She notices Bernard and excuses herself.

420. CU of Raymond, drinking champagne. Marion, crossing past him and then turning to him.

MARION: Excuse me. So, Raymond, it all worked out, didn't it.

421. Resume on Bernard, still watching Marion.

RAYMOND (*off-screen*): Yes. Very well. Except for Daxiat.

422. Raymond and Marion, as in 420. Marion turns toward Bernard and crosses right to him.

MARION: What are you doing all alone in a corner, Bernard?
BERNARD: Nothing. I was thinking about the play. And I wanted to tell you how extraordinary it is to work with you. Really, I was very moved.
MARION: I don't know how I was, but I thought you were wonderful.
BERNARD: Oh, I don't know. It will be better in two or three days.
MARION (*turning right, then back to Bernard*): Please, Bernard, help me. Do you see that man standing there?

423. Bernardini enters, peering around.

BERNARD (*off-screen*): Which one? The one who's by himself?
MARION (*off-screen*): Yes. I want him to leave. I don't want to see him.
Please.

424. Resume on Bernard and Marion.

BERNARD: O.K. Just a minute. Excuse me. (*Bernard crosses right as camera follows him. He approaches Bernardini.*) Good evening, Monsieur.
BERNARDINI: Good evening. You remember me?
BERNARD (*beginning to force Bernardini left across the stage to the exit*): Yes, of course. I want to say that you cannot stay here because this is a private gathering, a meeting.
BERNARDINI: Yes, but Madame Steiner is expecting me.
BERNARD: No, she isn't expecting anyone. She's exhausted. She sends her regrets. The exit is this way.
BERNARDINI: I'd like to know if she got my flowers, at least.
BERNARD: Your flowers? Let's talk about them.

425. Marion, watching Bernardini and Bernard, escapes off to the right.

BERNARD (*off-screen*): There were so many thorns that Madame Steiner's hands were bloody.
BERNARDINI: What?
BERNARD: Oh yes, absolutely. If I were in your shoes, I'd go right home.

426. BERNARD (*in the doorway, waving good-bye to Bernardini*): Quickly, quickly. Good-bye. Good-bye.

Bernard reenters and passes left along the same group of well-wishers we saw with Marion. As he passes Arlette, she kisses his cheek.

ARLETTE: Bravo, Bernard. You were terrific.
BERNARD: Thanks.

Bernard continues to the left until he comes to Germaine.

GERMAINE: Who are you looking for, my friend?
BERNARD: No one. I'm not looking for anyone.

Camera slowly lowers to the vent, cutting the characters out of frame.

MERLIN (*off-screen*): So, Germaine, you must be happy.
GERMAINE (*off-screen*): I'm happy for Marion above all.

427. The cellar. Shot begins on Marion, entering the foreground.

MARION: But after all, Lucas, we won them over. I don't understand you. You heard the applause, didn't you? We won them over.

Lucas enters from the right. Camera follows as he passes the dinner table, where he puts on his spectacles and picks up his notes.

LUCAS: Yes, we won them over, we won them over. But still it was far from perfect, let me tell you. From down here you can tell much better what didn't work. (*Lucas crosses right to the work table. He instructs Marion to sit at the left of the table, while he seats himself at the right.*) Well, first of all . . .
MARION: Come on, you must be crazy. You're not going to read me all that. The others are waiting for me. They'll wonder where I am. I can't stay so long.
LUCAS: Then I want you to come back later.
MARION: Later when? Look, we're up there all together. Lucas, you know how it is. I just can't leave like that.
LUCAS: Then come back tonight at least.
MARION (*crossing left*): No, it's not possible. Be sensible. I'll come see you tomorrow morning before the others get here.
LUCAS (*crossing to Marion as camera pulls back slightly*): At least take my notes. You can study them.
MARION: O.K. (*She takes the notes, folds them, then realizes that there is no place in her costume to hide them.*) But where can I put them? No, you keep them. (*She crosses back to the writing table.*) We'll look at them together tomorrow. O.K.? (*Lucas has followed Marion back to the writing table.*)

Kiss me. (*Lucas turns away from Marion and stares down at the notes on the table. Marion kisses him on the cheek and crosses left, out of frame.*) See you tomorrow.

Camera holds on Lucas, who watches Marion's exit. Various voices are heard from upstairs. Glancing at his notes, Lucas, with camera following him, crosses right, then turns around the corner toward the hole in the wall of the flue. Standing before the hole, listening to the voices, he removes his scarf and stuffs it into the hole. The last voice heard (off-screen) was that of

JEAN-LOUP: There you are, Marion. Where have you been? Get some champagne.

Fade to black.

428. MARION (*in* MS *at a newspaper kiosk*): Good morning, Monsieur

L'Orange. Do you have *Le Petit Parisien*, *Aujourd'hui*, *La Gerbe*, *Comoedia*, and (*pausing slightly*) *Je suis partout*?

429. The cellar. CU *of a newspaper column, headed "At the Theater." It is a review of* The Vanished One.

MARION (*off-screen*): This is Daxiat's article. "The Théâtre Montmartre, which has changed its management but not . . ."

430 to 442. Alternating shots of Marion, seated in MS *range at the dining table, and Lucas, hanging his laundry on a makeshift line.*

MARION: ". . . its orientation, has chosen to present us with a foggy Scandinavian vignette." "Foggy?" Naturally—he walked in fifteen minutes after the beginning.
LUCAS: Naturally.
MARION: "It is determinedly colorless and apolitical, while the real problems of our times are nowhere mentioned."
LUCAS: I knew it.
MARION: "Madame Steiner has not wished to break with the tradition of Jewish nihilism" (*Marion glances at Lucas*) "which for a long time shed disgrace on the prewar stage of the Théâtre Montmartre. But, you might say, there is nothing Jewish about *The Vanished One*. That is true. But everything is Jewified. Don't expect me to mention the staging credited to Jean-Loup Cottins. It is nothing more than an effeminate copy of what Lucas Steiner for so long inflicted upon us."
LUCAS: What do you know?
MARION: "As for the acting" (*she again glances at Lucas*) "what can we say about Marion Steiner except that she lavishes upon us her sad little expressions, and that she recites to herself in little bits and pieces as she was taught to do in the movies? Go back to the screen, Madame Steiner."
LUCAS (*pointing to Marion*): See?
MARION: Well! "Only a promising young man, Bernard Granger . . ."
LUCAS: What do you know?
MARION: ". . . imported from the Grand Guignol, creates a believable character. A star is born."
LUCAS: All the same . . . (*He laughs.*)

MARION: You think that's funny?

443. LUCAS (*crossing right to the writing table*): No, I don't think it's funny.
But the other reviews are good. There's nothing to complain about. And when
I see the advance sales, I know the run is assured. (*He sits, then picks up the
accounting sheet from the bed.*) We can thank you for that, Marion. Obviously.
(*He replaces the sheet on the bed and begins to dry his hands and button his
cuffs.*) Since you don't make movies anymore, people have to go to the theater
to see you.

*444 to 447. Alternating shots of Marion, as in the preceding series, and of
Lucas, as at the end of 443.*

MARION (*rereading*): ". . . the tradition of Jewish nihilism for a long time
    shed disgrace on the prewar stage of the Théâtre Montmartre." His name is
    right here: "Daxiat." But I feel as if I had just received an anonymous letter.
LUCAS: You're right. Daxiat and his friends have the same motives as those
    who write anonymous letters. Before the war they were nobody. And
    now . . .

448. Shot picks up on Lucas, as in the preceding series.

LUCAS: . . . they govern the country. But for how long? (*Lucas rises and
    moves left, behind the hanging laundry, to a table covered with books, one
    of which he picks up to show to Marion.*) Look at this book I'm reading.
    You're mentioned in it.

449. Resume on MARION: Me?

LUCAS (*enters frame, passes behind Marion, puts his arm around her, and
    holds the book before her*): Yes. Look. "Not content with monopolizing our
    theaters, the Jews take our most beautiful women." (*Camera begins to pull
    in on Marion and Lucas.*) Our most beautiful women.

Marion looks away. Fade to black.

450. A restaurant. Entering in foreground, a couple notes the loud singing that fills the room and is told by the headwaiter that a cast party is in progress. Camera moves right, to reveal the entire Théâtre Montmartre company singing vigorously at their table. Camera settles on the headwaiter, who has passed to right of frame beside a staircase, as a waiter descends and whispers something to him. The headwaiter nods and passes left to the Théâtre Montmartre table, pausing before Bernard who sits next to Marion against the wall.

HEADWAITER: Monsieur Granger, the director of the Théâtre Hébertot would like to speak with you.

Bernard protests, but is urged on by Marion. Germaine, at the head of the table, rises to let Bernard pass. Camera follows Bernard and the headwaiter up the flight of stairs (past a large photograph of Marshal Pétain).[30]

451. Bernard and the headwaiter are near the top of the stairs. The headwaiter gestures toward the left. Camera follows Bernard as he crosses left toward a full table. Bernard presents himself to the director of the Hébertot, who in turn introduces him to various diners, including Daxiat, who is seated with his back to camera.[31]

DAXIAT: My dear Granger, bravo! I'm delighted to be able to congratulate you. It was a fantastic performance.
BERNARD: Monsieur, what you have done is unspeakable.
DAXIAT: What are you referring to?
BERNARD: You will make your excuses to Madame Steiner immediately.
DAXIAT: You must be joking. That is out of the question.
BERNARD (*passing right, around the corner of the table, and standing before Daxiat*): Not at all, Monsieur. And to the other actors of *The Vanished One* as well.

Bernard pulls Daxiat up by his lapels.

DAXIAT (*standing*): I won't fight here.
BERNARD: Then we'll fight outside.

Bernard again seizes Daxiat by his lapels and forces him to the top of the stairway, then part of the way down.

DAXIAT: You're insane! What is this?

452. Bernard continues to force Daxiat down the stairs, Daxiat all the while continuing his protestations.

DAXIAT: This is incredible. You are ridiculous, my good man. Goddamn it!

They arrive at the foot of the stairs, near the Théâtre Montmartre table.

BERNARD: You'll make your excuses to Madame Steiner.

Daxiat attempts to walk past the table to the exit. Bernard runs after him, as those at the table rise and cry out for Bernard to stop. Bernard catches Daxiat, turns him around, and points him toward Marion.

BERNARD: Make your excuses!
DAXIAT: I have nothing to excuse myself for. I was just doing my job.
MARION: Bernard!

Marion and the others leave the table to follow as Bernard catches hold of Daxiat's lapel and pulls him toward the exit.

453. The doorway of the restaurant, seen from the outside. It is pouring. In MLS *range, Bernard pulls Daxiat through the doorway, then releases him. As Daxiat continues to protest that he will not fight, Bernard again lunges at Daxiat's lapels and drags him down the few steps to the street. In the street, the argument continues.*

DAXIAT: You're wasting your time. I tell you that I won't fight.

Daxiat tries to move up the street out of Bernard's clutches.

BERNARD (*pursuing Daxiat*): And I tell you that you will.
DAXIAT (*turning to face Bernard*): I'm not a boxer, sir, I'm a journalist.

Bernard again grabs Daxiat by the lapels and throws him against a car. Daxiat slips and falls to the ground, dropping his walking stick, which Bernard picks up and flings off-screen.

454. The restaurant doorway. The Théâtre Montmartre company rushes out. Merlin, Raymond, and Marc run after Bernard and Daxiat; Marion wants to join them, but is restrained by the other members of the company.

455. Resume on the street. Merlin and Marc help Daxiat up from the ground while Raymond tries to restrain Bernard. Then all but Bernard pass out of frame left in the direction of the restaurant.

DAXIAT: This is absolutely intolerable. Leave me alone. Leave me alone. I want to make a phone call. Where is the telephone?

Bernard alone on the street, now also passes left and runs into Marion.

MARION (*furious*): You're irresponsible. You're an animal. What in the world did you think you were doing?

456. The window of the restaurant. Several employees peer out at the street.

457. Resume on Marion and Bernard, now in CS range.

MARION (*shouting*): Did you stop to think about the theater for one moment? What if the play is banned? What if the theater is requisitioned?
BERNARD (*grabbing Marion and whirling her around*): All you care about is your theater. Will it be sold out tomorrow? Are the discount tickets selling? Will we be able to do an extra show on Christmas? There are other places full these days. Prisons, for example.
MARION (*crossing left and catching Bernard by his lapels*): Listen to me. We're in the same boat. We have to continue working together. But outside of that, I don't ever want you to speak to me again.

458. The restaurant window. Daxiat watches the scene between Marion and Bernard.

459. Marion runs up the steps into the restaurant. Bernard remains alone on the street. He rubs his wet head, turns, and walks away from camera. He again turns around and shoves his hands in his pockets. Suddenly, on the soundtrack:

BERNARD (*off-screen*): "You are beautiful, Helena."

460. On stage, Bernard and Marion, in exact replica of 399, stand facing the audience.

BERNARD: "So beautiful, that to look at you is painful."
MARION: "Yesterday you said it was a joy."
BERNARD: "It is a joy. And a torment."

Applause.

461. MCS *of Raymond, pulling the curtains.*

462. MS *of Marion and Bernard, behind the closing curtains. As Bernard reaches for her hand, Marion jerks her arm away.*

463. Marion and Bernard, seen from the audience's perspective, step through the opened curtain to bow, then step back; again, Marion rejects Bernard's hand.

464. CU *of a small package. A hand opens it and removes a miniature casket. The casket is opened; a small noose is removed from it. Camera pulls back: it is Jean-Loup who has opened the package.*

JEAN-LOUP (*holding up the noose to show it to Merlin*): It's incredible. It's crazy.

465. The cellar. From shot of the table top covered with potatoes, camera lifts to show Marion, standing and peeling potatoes.

MARION: You see, Lucas, the play runs by itself. You have no more instructions to give us.

466. Lucas, in his spectacles, reclining, a book in front of him.

MARION (*off-screen*): Why are you giving me such a mean look?

467. MARION (MCU): Sometimes I think you hate me.

468. Resume on Lucas, as in 466.

LUCAS: No, of course not. It would be crazy to hate you.

He starts to remove his spectacles.

469. Resume on Marion, as in 467.

MARION: But you are a little crazy. I know you well.

470. Resume on Lucas.

LUCAS: I know you well, too. (*He rises, looking at Marion.*) As far as I'm
concerned, *The Vanished One* belongs to the past. I have another idea. *The
Magic Mountain.*[32] (*He moves left to stand before a large chart, on which
his ideas for the production are taking shape.*) There will be a role for you.
It fits you like a glove. (*He looks at Marion.*) Are you listening to me?

471 to 478. Alternating shots of Marion and Lucas, as last seen.

MARION: Yes, I'm listening.
LUCAS: This is it. There is a cruel woman.
MARION: Cruel? Me?
LUCAS: I'm talking about the character. Yes, she's kind, tender, even loving,
    and yet she's cruel without really being aware of it. Without wishing to be.
    She's cruel in spite of herself.
MARION: Cruel?
LUCAS: It will be wonderful. You'll see. I'm going to have you speak without
    literary affectation, using ordinary language. I'll use your own expressions.
    Do you understand?

479. MARION (*now in much closer range*): Yes. What I understand above all is
that from now on all I say may be used against me.

Slow fade to black.

480. The offices of Je suis partout. *The sound of printing presses is heard
throughout the shot.*

Jean-Loup enters a doorway from the street. Pausing to ask directions, he moves past the presses, files, etc., until he reaches a woman standing at a pile of newspapers with her back to camera.

JEAN-LOUP: Is Monsieur Daxiat's office over there?
WOMAN: His is the first office on the right.

Camera holds on Jean-Loup as he passes through a doorway. Framed in the doorway, he is joined by Daxiat. Together they return toward camera, then turn to frame right.

481. MS of Jean-Loup and Daxiat.

JEAN-LOUP: I confess that I was somewhat reluctant to come. Coming from someone like you, it's hard to tell whether it's an invitation or an order.
DAXIAT: I see you misread my review.
JEAN-LOUP: Was it really a review? I had the feeling it was more like revenge.
DAXIAT: Even if it was revenge, it wasn't directed against you. On the contrary.

A young woman enters, carrying the mock layout of the next edition.

JEAN-LOUP: On the contrary?
DAXIAT: Yes. Excuse me.
JEAN-LOUP: Of course.
DAXIAT: Is it four o'clock already? (*to Jean-Loup*) Pardon me.
JEAN-LOUP: Naturally.

Camera follows Daxiat and the woman as they move back to a high-backed desk, where they post the layout. Daxiat makes some corrections, then returns to his original position opposite Jean-Loup.

DAXIAT: Yes, when I went to the theater the other night, I thought I would see a play staged by Jean-Loup Cottins. (*Daxiat takes a few steps away from camera, then returns.*) Instead, I saw a nondescript show, without a style of its own. In short, I had the feeling that you were a front, and what's worse, a front for someone who isn't here.

JEAN-LOUP: If I were in a good mood, I'd say that I would speak to you only in the presence of my lawyer. (*He extends his hand to Daxiat.*) But I'd rather just leave.

DAXIAT: Wait. Wait a moment. I haven't yet gotten to the point. I have a proposition for you.

JEAN-LOUP: Whatever it is, I can say no right away.

DAXIAT: I want you to help me save the Théâtre Montmartre.

482. Over-the-shoulder CU *of Jean-Loup.*

DAXIAT: You know that Lucas Steiner left the theater to his wife before leaving. Well, we have proof that the sale was not legal because the transfer was predated.

483. DAXIAT (CU): This kind of transaction has a name: "false aryanization."

JEAN-LOUP (*off-screen*): Yes, and so . . . ?

DAXIAT: So, that means that legally the Théâtre Montmartre belongs to no one and the Germans can requisition it from one day to the next. Unless . . .

JEAN-LOUP (*off-screen*): Unless?

DAXIAT: Unless the direction is taken over by someone who is acceptable to them.

484. The cellar. Camera holds close on Marion throughout, pulling back slightly as Lucas, polishing a shoe, passes in front of her.

MARION: You see, Daxiat didn't beat around the bush with Jean-Loup. He proposed quite simply that they share in the direction of the theater. Daxiat would choose the plays and Jean-Loup would stage them.

LUCAS: I'm certain that Jean-Loup turned him down.

MARION: No, of course he didn't turn him down. He couldn't. He could only put him off, and so he asked for time to think it over. The only way to fight Daxiat is to appeal to someone above him: Doktor Dietrich, if necessary. But Jean-Loup doesn't want to set foot in the Propaganda Bureau any more.

485. The Propaganda Bureau. A Nazi flag dominates the frame. Throughout, various officers are paged over the loudspeaker. At the right stands a German soldier. Marion enters from the left.

MARION: I have an appointment with Doktor Dietrich.
SOLDIER: Next floor. You ask the orderly.

Marion turns left and enters the elevator. Another soldier calls to her, takes her by the arm, and leads her out of the elevator, which a Nazi officer then enters.

SOLDIER: Careful, Madame. You'll take the elevator in a moment, Madame.

Camera follows as Marion crosses right to a double stairway. A German officer offers Marion a glass of champagne; she says nothing. As she ascends the right flight, Martine, on the arm of a German officer, descends the left.

486 to 490. Alternating CUS of Marion and Martine, staring sidelong at each other as the one ascends and the other descends.

491. LS of Marion as she reaches the top of the stairway. Camera follows as she turns to frame left and pauses before an orderly seated at a desk.

MARION: I want to see Doktor Dietrich.
ORDERLY: Impossible, Madame.
MARION: But I spoke with him yesterday by phone. He is expecting me.
ORDERLY: What is your name?
MARION: Marion Steiner.
ORDERLY (*glancing at his calendar*): Yes, you have an appointment at five
    o'clock. But it is impossible.

A German officer appears from an office doorway behind Marion, crosses right, exits frame, then reenters.

MARION: Why is that? I can wait.
ORDERLY: I'm terribly sorry, Madame, but there is no point in waiting. Doktor
    Dietrich has left for the Eastern front. He has rejoined his combat unit.
MARION: That's that.

Camera follows as Marion recrosses to the right. As she passes the officer, he follows her.

OFFICER: Madame Steiner, I would like to speak with you.

Marion follows the officer to the doorway next to the one from which he emerged. They enter.

492. Interior of the office. Marion glances around. The officer, whose left arm is in a sling, takes his place at frame left.

OFFICER: Madame Steiner, I am a great admirer. Allow me to introduce myself. I am Lieutenant Bergen.

493 to 495. Alternating over-the-shoulder shots of Marion and Bergen.

BERGEN: You wish to see Doktor Dietrich?
MARION: Yes.
BERGEN: He hasn't left for the Eastern front. Tonight he put a bullet through his head in his room at the Hôtel Raphael.

Marion lowers her eyes.

496. CU *of Bergen's hand reaching for Marion's.*

BERGEN: Very sad.

497 to 509. Alternating CUs *of Bergen, Marion, and Bergen's hand grasping Marion's. By the end of this series of very quick shots, Marion is looking around in desperation.*

BERGEN: Doktor Dietrich admired you very much. And I admire you too, very much. I am very honored to shake your hand, Madame.

510. LS *of the office. As a soldier enters one door, Bergen releases Marion's hand and she flees through another door.*

511 to 523. Inside a church. This series of shots is completely without dialogue. On the soundtrack is heard, repeated, the patriotic "Hymn to

Mercy" as sung by a boys' choir (which we soon see). The hymn ends with
the repeated phrase "Save, save France, in the name of the Sacred Heart."
    Bernard enters the church from the left, removes his hat, pauses, passes
before an altar as he crosses right, and pauses again beside the boys' choir,
which is being rehearsed by a priest. Bernard crosses in front of the choir;
then, in close range, he is seen carefully looking about, his eye fixing first
on an area of confessional booths, then on a woman, recently come from the
direction of the confessionals, lighting a candle. A man in black, hat in hand,
enters the church, pauses, then walks down the aisle toward camera. Bernard
looks at his wristwatch. Christian enters the church at the rear, followed by
a man in black. This man crosses behind Christian, glancing back at him;
Christian returns the glance. Bernard crosses back past the choirboys and
faces Christian. Christian proceeds down the aisle toward the altar as Bernard
smiles and moves forward to meet him. Christian makes a small warning
gesture to Bernard. Christian and Bernard cross paths on the aisle. Christian
arrives at the altar, then quickly turns left, toward the door through which
Bernard had entered. Abruptly, Christian turns in the opposite direction,
toward the confessionals, then back. He begins to run down the aisle, toward
camera. From several directions, three men rush toward Christian; he retreats,
and with the men walks from the church through the door at the front. Bernard,
watching all this, leaves by the door at the rear.

524. Outside the church. Bernard sees the men forcing Christian into a waiting
car, which pulls away and around a corner as Bernard looks on.

525. Marion's dressing room. She is seen from the rear seated at her make-up
table, her reflection in the mirror before us. Bernard enters, seen first in the
mirror.

BERNARD: I'd like to speak with you. I'm terribly sorry, Madame Steiner, but
I really must speak with you. I'm going to give up the theater. (He moves to
frame left, beside the table.) I'll turn my part over in a month or so, however
long it takes you to find a replacement.
MARION: Of course, of course. I should have known this would happen.

Camera follows as Bernard paces about the room, ending up once more beside
the table, this time at frame right, with Marion facing him.

BERNARD: No, it's not at all what you think. I know you are very angry with me
   since the fight with Daxiat and I understand your reaction completely. Completely. Even if you don't speak to me anymore, and if you avoid my glance, we
   perform together every night, and I must tell you that I like the play—and my
   role in it—more and more. From that point of view, I'm quite happy, believe me.
MARION: You don't need to explain. You're free. I'm not even sure we'll be
   looking for a replacement. In a month the theater may be closed. In any
   case, I'm sure that you have a better offer at the Hébertot or . . .
BERNARD (*crossing to the left side of the table*): Not at all. Not at all. I'm not
   thinking of going to the Hébertot or anywhere else. It's just that I'm leaving
   the theater temporarily . . . for the Resistance.

*Marion turns to look at Bernard, then suddenly rises and slaps him violently
across the face.*

*526 to 542. During this sequence, shots of the performance of the play are
intercut with shots of a developing drama backstage. For the sake of clarity,
the two will here be outlined separately.*

526 and 539 are ELS *views of the audience.*

527, 529, 531, 532, 535, 537, 540, and 542 are on stage, the actors seen from various angles and at various distances. But even as they perform The Vanished One, *they turn to peer off-stage, aware that something is wrong. Indeed, during 529 Marion, taking advantage of an exit within the play, hurries off to confer with Raymond and reenters the play only in 542. The text of the play, a few sections of which, heard from off-screen, are indecipherable, runs as follows.*

JEAN-LOUP: "Helena, if you don't mind. I want to speak with Monsieur Carl alone."

MARION: "But if it's about Eric, after all, I have the right to know what you are saying."

JEAN-LOUP: "Of course, of course, Helena."

MARION: ". . . but after all, Monsieur Carl, do you think this is right? I'm Eric's mother and yet I don't have the right to know what decisions are being made for my son."

BERNARD: "Frankly speaking, Doctor Sanders, I find this situation terribly embarrassing. Don't you think that—"

JEAN-LOUP: "No, please, Monsieur Carl. Now Helena, I beg you to leave us alone."

MARION: "All right. Since I am not welcome in this house."

She exits.

JEAN-LOUP: "Well, this is the whole story. It was the twenty-fourth of October. Helena went out for a walk in the garden and suddenly she disappeared . . . Two weeks later she reappeared, pale as a ghost, unable to say what happened."

BERNARD: "Do you mean she had amnesia?"

JEAN-LOUP: "Yes, in a way. Then the child was born."

BERNARD: "Don't you think the child . . ."

JEAN-LOUP: "You are absolutely right, but Helena bears me a degree of affection that may appear excessive in the eyes of strangers. She has moments of expansiveness toward me that resemble those of a little girl. I don't know why she overflows with gratitude toward me."

BERNARD: "She often seems excessively humble."
JEAN-LOUP: "No one will ever know what she feels guilty of, but the corruption which she feels within herself leads her to seek the affection of her inferiors. So, poor Charles-Henri didn't really understand what was happening and that was the tragedy."
MARION (*reentering*): "Who is talking of tragedy here?"

Applause.

Meanwhile, during 527 we hear Raymond, off-screen, inquiring: "What's this?" *In 528, we see Raymond disputing with two men, one of whom shows an I.D. and announces* Civil Defense, *the other of whom says:* "We've come to inspect the cellar." *In 530, we see one of these "Civil Defense" agents framed in the doorway: he is one of the men we saw capturing Christian in the church sequence above, 511 to 523; in 533 and 536 we see both agents in the doorway. In 534, we see Raymond and Marion talking backstage.*

RAYMOND: They want to inspect the cellar.

MARION: Inspect the cellar?
RAYMOND: Yes.
MARION: That's out of the question.

Then, in 538, we turn to Raymond and Marion. Marion says "Put them in a side loge" and exits as the agents enter. Raymond tells the agents "Follow me, but don't make any noise," and leads them off behind the set, where we see Raymond and the agents through a break in the wall of the set. (We also see Marion through this break, preparing for her next stage entrance.) Later, in 539, we again glimpse the agents backstage. In 541, we see a side loge. Raymond opens the door at the rear, looks around, and withdraws; the two agents enter and stand behind the seated spectators.

543 to 545. A series of quick shots of off-stage activities: Raymond closes the curtains, two stagehands move furniture, Raymond gestures for a new scene to begin.

546. The side loge. The agents, in MS, *stand behind the spectators.*

BERNARD (*off-screen*): "I have proof that Doctor Sanders . . ."

547. On stage. Bernard and Marion, in her tattered costume.

BERNARD: ". . . didn't return the day after, but the day before, the death of Charles-Henri."

Marion gasps and faints.

548. On the darkened stage, Bernard helps Marion up from the floor and over to the couch.

BERNARD: Do you know those two guys?
MARION: They're from the Civil Defense.
BERNARD: No. They're from the Gestapo. I'm sure of it. I know one of them.

549. The agents, as in 546.

550. Resume on Marion and Bernard.

MARION: From the Gestapo?
BERNARD: Yes, yes.
MARION: If I ask you to help me, will you?
BERNARD: Yes.
MARION: Without any questions?
BERNARD: Yes.

551. Backstage. Shot begins on Raymond, following the play with his script; then camera lowers to the vent.

BERNARD (*off-screen*): "Love is painful. Like a great bird of prey, it hovers above us, then stops and threatens us. But in this threat there may also be a promise of happiness."

552. On stage. Once more, the closing lines of the play are spoken; this time Bernard and Marion are seen in MCS.

BERNARD: "You are beautiful, Helena. So beautiful that to look at you is painful."
MARION: "Yesterday you told me it was a joy."
BERNARD: "It's a joy. And a torment."

Bernard places his hands on Marion's shoulders; the curtain closes in front of them.

553. The side loge. The agents are now seen in closer range.

554. On stage. Marion peers warily through the opening in the curtain.

555. The side loge. The agents open the door and exit.

556. Backstage. Camera begins on Marion in CU, *then follows her as she passes around Raymond, tears off her wig and hands it to Germaine, and exits through the rear doorway, followed by Bernard.*

MARION: No curtain calls and no bows tonight.
GERMAINE (*off-screen*): What's going on, Raymond?
RAYMOND (*off-screen*): No curtain calls and no bows. A couple of guys from the Civil Defense are here.

557. The two agents make their way backstage and toward the rear stairway to the second floor. They pass the trapdoor just as Marion and Bernard are closing it behind them on their way to the cellar.

558. The cellar. Lucas, in MCU, *stands working on his* Magic Mountain *chart. Hearing footsteps, he turns, begins to smile, then abruptly stops. Camera pulls back as Marion and Bernard enter.*

MARION: Lucas, this is Bernard Granger. Bernard, this is my husband.

As Bernard stares at Lucas in amazement, camera follows Marion left as she steps on a stool to look over the partition—presumably left over from some struck set—that serves Lucas for one wall. She descends, crosses past Bernard and Lucas to the bed, grabs two pillows, recrosses the room, and throws the pillows over the partition. As she crosses back, she pauses between Bernard and Lucas.

MARION: Don't stand there like statues. You have five minutes to get rid of everything and hide.

Marion moves left; Bernard and Lucas stare first at her, then at each other, and go to work clearing the room.

559. Near the "Administration" offices. In MS, *Raymond and the two Gestapo agents argue.*

FIRST AGENT: We've waited long enough. Take us to the cellar.
RAYMOND (*holding on to the agent*): No, no. Madame Steiner has the key.

Marc in his gamekeeper's costume enters the corridor. The first agent watches him, then turns back to Raymond.

FIRST AGENT: I'm going to speak with Madame Steiner myself.
RAYMOND: No, no. You're making a mistake. She's undressing. Please.

560. *The stairway to the second floor. Marion rushes toward camera, then left in the foreground, in front of the agents. Raymond and the agents continue to argue.*

FIRST AGENT: What's going on here?
RAYMOND: I guess I made a mistake.
FIRST AGENT: We've waited long enough.
RAYMOND: Here she comes.
MARION (*emerging from the "Administration" door*): Three minutes, gentlemen, please give me three minutes.
RAYMOND: So there you are.

561. *The hallway outside the door to the cellar. Raymond, with a lantern, leads Marion and the agents through the door and down the steps.*

RAYMOND: I haven't been down here in a long time. I'm warning you that it may be full of rats. Do you have the key, Madame Steiner?
MARION: Yes, yes I do.
RAYMOND: Thanks. Watch your heads, please.

562. The cellar. Raymond, lighting a lamp hanging on the wall, continues to lead the procession.

RAYMOND: Here we are. I don't know much about these things but I don't think it's deep enough for a shelter down here. There are hardly eight inches between the ceiling and the pavement of the courtyard.

As the group moves toward camera, then left, we see the cellar utterly transformed, with no signs of any recent habitation. The agents begin to poke around.

FIRST AGENT: What's this?
RAYMOND: It's the screen we used in *The Cherry Orchard.*

563. The faces of Lucas and Bernard, peering through a hole in the "wall" behind which they are hiding in the boiler area.

FIRST AGENT (*off-screen*): It can hold thirty-five to forty people, not more.

564. Resume on Marion, Raymond, and the agents, as at the end of 562.

MARION: In any case, because of the humidity it was declared unhealthy in 1939.
FIRST AGENT: And what do you do in case of an alert?
RAYMOND: In case of an alert we have the right to take refuge in the subway.
MARION: The local station stays open all night for that purpose.

The four begin to pass out of view to the left.

RAYMOND: Say, Madame Steiner, that staircase there, couldn't we burn it? We could use it for firewood.
MARION: Yes, fine, Raymond.

The first agent takes one last long look around the cellar.

565. Through a vertical break in the "wall" we see Marion and the inspection party leaving the cellar.

RAYMOND: In any case, there are so many alerts now that people won't go down to the shelters any more.

566. Bernard and Lucas in almost complete darkness, trying to make their way out of their hiding place.

LUCAS: That's that. They're gone until the next time.
BERNARD: Being shut up down here is no life.
LUCAS: It is a life. It's my life.
BERNARD: Couldn't a better hiding place be found, a safer one?
LUCAS: I'm not looking for a hiding place. This is my home. And no one will make me leave.

The candles they have lit now clearly illuminate both their faces. Bernard begins to move toward camera, Lucas following.

LUCAS: Tell me, do you think my wife is beautiful? I want to ask you a question, Bernard. (*He slowly turns his back to camera to face Bernard.*) She's in love with you. Are you in love with her?

Camera holds on Bernard, who turns away from Lucas. In so doing, he notices with surprise the hole in the wall of the flue.

567. The director's table in the orchestra. Jean-Loup sits watching still another rehearsal of The Vanished One.

MARION (*off-screen*): "Now I'm coming to love, Carl. And it hurts. Does love hurt?"

568. On stage. Marc stands at the left with a copy of the script; in the background at the right sit Raymond and Germaine, watching. A new young actor is now playing Carl. And the rehearsal is viewed from a new perspective, from the side of the stage. Marc directs the new actor upstage, then downstage toward Marion.

YOUNG ACTOR: "Yes, love hurts. Like great birds of prey, it hovers over us. It stops and threatens us, but in this threat is also a promise of happiness. You are beautiful, Helena, so beautiful that to look at you is painful."
MARION: "Yesterday you told me it was a joy."
YOUNG ACTOR: "It's a joy. And a torment."

569. MCS *of Bernard, from whose point of view on the stage we have been watching the preceding shot. Slowly, he turns and leaves the stage.*

570. *Camera holds on the open doorway of Bernard's dressing room, then follows Marion as she enters. Bernard is removing his photographs, posters, etc., from the walls and placing them in a pile on a table. During the course of the shot, Marion will occasionally help Bernard in this chore. The two will come together, look at and look away from each other, as the camera freely follows their various movements.*

MARION: Bernard, may I speak with you? If I hadn't come to your dressing room, you would have left without saying good-bye.
BERNARD: Not at all. I was waiting for the rehearsal to end.
MARION: It's ended. It was sad.
BERNARD: Yes, I looked in for a moment.
MARION: And?
BERNARD: It was good. A little lesson in humility. One realizes that one can be replaced.
MARION (*moving to the door*): Well, good-bye then, Bernard.

She extends her hand.

Bernard approaches Marion and takes her hand, but then pushes the door closed and kisses her. Marion touches Bernard's face, then turns away.

MARION: I had the feeling that you were interested in all women . . . except me.

BERNARD: First of all, not all women. And secondly, you frightened me.
Sometimes you looked at me severely, and even with a certain hostility.

MARION: With a certain hostility? Really?

BERNARD: Yes, I swear. I felt you were judging me.

MARION: It was quite the opposite. You aroused feelings in me . . . Yes,
feelings, truly you did. And since I thought everyone would see it on my
face, I tried to hide it. And you came to hate me.

BERNARD: That's not true. I never hated you. But I didn't understand why you
had become so distant after that kiss.

MARION: Everyone kisses in the theater.

BERNARD: Not necessarily on the mouth.

MARION: I kissed you on the mouth?

BERNARD: Yes. On opening night. During the curtain call.

MARION: No, no. That's not possible.

BERNARD: You kissed me on the mouth.

He moves close to Marion and takes her hand, palm up, and lowers his head to kiss it.

MARION: Aren't you going to tell me that there are two women in me?
BERNARD: Yes, exactly. There are two women in you. A married woman who doesn't love her husband anymore.
MARION: No. You're wrong about that. Don't try to guess. You can't understand.

571. Throughout this shot, camera remains generally closer to Bernard and Marion than in the preceding shot. Bernard, first seen in CU, moves to his make-up table, where he picks up a hairbrush and razor and places them in a traveling case on the table. Marion brings a box of greasepaints and another of powder, and places them on top of the case.

MARION: You mustn't forget your make-up.
BERNARD (*removing the boxes to the make-up table*): Don't bother. I'm going to leave it for my replacement. (*He returns to Marion.*) Where I'm going, I won't need make-up.
MARION: But you may need a disguise.

Bernard places his hand on Marion's cheek; she removes the hand from her face but does not release it.

BERNARD: I'm sorry. I'm sorry.

They begin to kiss, passionately. Finally they drop to the floor, where Marion's bare legs are seen under the table as Bernard lies on top of her.

MARION: Yes. Yes. Yes. Yes. Yes. Yes.

572. On stage. Over a MS of Bernard's replacement and Marion, the following voice-over (not heard since the opening montage of the film) begins.

VOICE-OVER: After the departure of Bernard, *The Vanished One* continued with Lucien Ballard in the role of Carl.
MARION: "No, be quiet. You have no right."

573. MS *of Nadine, on stage. She exits from a door of the set into the wings, where she winks and crosses to Germaine, who helps her on with her coat. Nadine then crosses right toward the stage door, where a chauffeur stands.*

JACQUOT (*off-screen*): "Is Monsieur Carl going to return?"
VOICE-OVER: Nadine Marsac, headed for fame, rushes off each night after speaking her last line. A chauffeur waits for her in the wings. He drives her to the Billancourt studios, where *The Angels of Mercy* is being shot at night. She has the leading role.

574. Nadine, smoking a cigarette, is being fitted in a wimple for her role as a nun in The Angels of Mercy. *The fitter is Arlette.*

VOICE-OVER: There she meets up again with Arlette Guillaume, who is in charge of the design of the sets and the costumes.

575 to 578. Documentary shots of the D Day landing, all superimposed on an ELS *of a theater audience.*

VOICE-OVER: On June 6, 1944, the Allied troops land in Normandy. Everyday life becomes more and more difficult for the Parisians.

579. ELS *of a theater audience.*

VOICE-OVER: And yet each night they crowd in greater numbers into movies and theaters.
NADINE (*off-screen*): "Isn't Master Eric with you, Madame?"

At the sound of an air-raid siren, the entire audience looks upward.

580. Shot of an air-raid siren.

581. Jean-Loup walks onstage and gestures helplessly to the audience.

582. Outside the Théâtre Montmartre. A crowd stands staring upward.

VOICE-OVER: One night, instead of seeking shelter in the subway station, the audience stands in the square to watch the ballet of English airplanes over the skies of Paris.

583 to 585. Three ELS *views of audiences rising and staring upward. Superimposed are the words* "THÉÂTRE DE LA CITÉ," "THÉÂTRE HÉBERTOT," "THÉÂTRE LA BRUYÈRE," *and* "THÉÂTRE DU GRAND GUIGNOL."

VOICE-OVER: The shutting-off of electricity forces many theaters to close.

586. On stage. Jacquot, writing his lessons, and Marion, doing needlepoint, sit at the table, playing their scene.

VOICE-OVER: The Montmartre stays open until July 9, thanks to Raymond's ingenuity.

Camera lowers and travels left along the floor toward the footlights—which are not footlights.

VOICE-OVER: He has the brilliant idea of replacing the footlights with a dozen automobile headlights.

Camera raises to show Raymond and Marc furiously pedaling their stationary bicycles, generating power for the headlights.

Fade to black.

VOICE-OVER: The German defeat is inevitable.

587. Lucas, guarding his eyes from the sun, emerges up the cellar stairs, aided by Marion.

VOICE-OVER: After 813 days and 813 nights in the cellar of his theater, Lucas can't wait to see the light of day.

588 to 598. Intercut with shots of shooting on the streets and rooftops of Paris are shots of Lucas reentering the outside world.

VOICE-OVER: It is one of those strange moments in which gunfire is exchanged from rooftops without anyone having a very clear idea of who is shooting at whom.

Lucas stares at the action in the streets. Marion pulls him back into the safety of the theater doorway. Lucas then edges against the outside wall of the theater. A workman carrying a pack of wine bottles crosses from frame right. A stray barrage of bullets shatters the bottles.

LUCAS: Are you all right?

The man runs into a doorway for protection.

LUCAS (*waving his finger*): No, not there, not there!

The man rushes from the doorway back to frame right. Lucas continues to walk along the front of the theater, arriving at last at a corner where sandbags are piled. Nearly hit by a stray bullet, Lucas flattens himself against the wall.

599. Jean-Loup, in a bathrobe, looking mildly exasperated, is escorted from the front door of his apartment building by three soldiers and led to a waiting jeep.

VOICE-OVER: Difficult times are beginning for Jean-Loup Cottins. Pulled out of his bed by some young members of the FFI,[33] he is taken to police headquarters, where he is freed that same night thanks to his connections.

600. Jean-Loup, in a bathrobe, looking mildly exasperated, is escorted from his front door by three soldiers. The camera is slightly closer.

VOICE-OVER: He is arrested a second time the next morning because of his connections.

601. ELS of the still-burning rubble of a bombed city, presumably Hamburg. Daxiat, wearing an eye-patch and a tattered coat, picks his way desperately through the rubble; shot ends with him stumbling toward a window from which flames shoot forth.

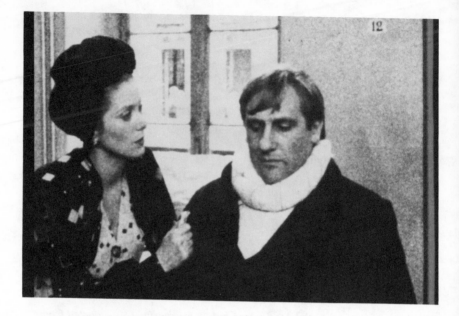

VOICE-OVER: Daxiat, on the other hand, will flee for his life. The columnist of *Je suis partout* has become a man without a country. He loses an eye in the terrible bombing of Hamburg. He follows Marshal Pétain to Sigmaringen for a while and then, via a succession of monasteries, he finally gets to Spain. Sentenced to death in absentia, he will die of throat cancer in the 1960s. But in that late summer of 1944, the war is not yet over, and our story is still awaiting its epilogue.

602. *A hospital ward. Marion, dressed in severe black and white, enters in* CS *range from the right and asks directions of a nurse. Camera follows as Marion passes through the crowded ward, past patients and nurses and visitors; then, asking directions of another nurse, she walks toward camera. She pauses for a long moment, then crosses left to Bernard, who sits in a wheelchair. She seats herself on a bed to the left.*

603. *Reaction shot of two nurses, who watch and whisper.*

604. Marion and Bernard in MS *range. Behind them, through a window and across the hospital courtyard, two figures are seen stirring in open windows.*

MARION: I tried to forget you. I couldn't. If it hadn't been for your stupid pride, I would have come to you long ago.
BERNARD: And in order to come, you would have had to invent a new lie each time.
MARION: Lie? Why lie? Lie to whom? Since he's dead.
BERNARD: You must have taken refuge in your work.

605 to 612. Alternating CUS *of Marion and Bernard. The background is blurred.*

MARION: No, I found suddenly that it was no longer of any interest to me. I gave it all up. Listen to me. I want just one thing. To be near you. To leave this place. I'm certain we can begin a new life.
BERNARD: No. We can't begin anything anew because there is nothing new to begin. There was never anything real between us. I played with the idea of loving you, but I didn't love you at all. Do you understand me? It was an abstraction. Of course, you had reason to believe I did, since I believed it myself.
MARION: But I never stopped thinking about you, not one single day.
BERNARD: Neither did I. I thought of you, but less and less frequently. And now I don't have any idea why you are here. I have forgotten your last name, your first name. I sense that by and by the features of your face will become completely indistinct. Go away. (*more insistently*) Go away.

613. Reaction shot of the two nurses.

614. CU *of Bernard. Camera at once begins to pull back so as to include Marion in frame. And as camera retreats, the background comes into focus: now it is a painted flat, of which the two figures in the window are a part.*

MARION: Listen to me. Listen carefully. It takes two to love just as it takes two to hate. And I will love you in spite of yourself. Just the thought of you makes my heart beat more quickly. That's all that counts for me. Farewell.

She rises, crosses behind Bernard, and exits. Camera again begins to pull back. Bernard buries his face in his hands. And curtains swish closed before camera.

615. ELS *pan of audience applauding.*

616. On stage. Bernard rises from his wheelchair and walks downstage to bow. He extends his hand to Marion, who enters from the right. The two now bow, and are joined by the two actresses playing the nurses, who take their places at either side of Bernard and Marion.

617. MS *of Lucas, sitting in his box, in the shadows.*

618. ELS *of audience. One man rises to cry "There's Lucas Steiner!"*

619. Lucas leans forward into the light. Voices are heard from the audience, recognizing his presence.

620. ELS *of the audience in the balcony, looking at Lucas and applauding.*

621. Lucas rises and bows. Voices of approval and of recognition continue to be heard.

622. Another ELS *of the applauding audience.*

623. On stage. Bernard whispers something to Marion, who smiles and nods. Bernard crosses right to the edge of the stage and reaches to Lucas in his box. Lucas steps onto the stage and joins Marion and Bernard as all three acknowledge the applause.

624. ELS *of the balcony audience, rising to its feet and applauding.*

625. CU *of Lucas, gesturing to the audience.*

626. CU *of Bernard, who looks first at Lucas, then at the audience, and grins.*

627. CU *of Marion, who turns her eyes to the right, then to the audience, then lowers her eyes. Again looking left, she crosses behind Bernard.*

628.   CU *of Marion's hand taking Bernard's, then a quick pan to Marion's other hand taking Lucas's.*

629.   CU *of Marion, smiling, bowing, looking first at Lucas, then at Bernard, then front. The frame freezes. An iris-in on Marion introduces the final credits, in which each of the major players is seen in an iris against a red background.*

Notes

1. Chambre des Députés. Site of the French parliament.
2. *La Symphonie fantastique* (1941), directed by Christian-Jaque, depicted the life of the nineteenth-century composer Hector Berlioz. Jean-Louis Barrault, who would portray another important romantic artist, the mime Baptiste in Marcel Carné's *Children of Paradise* (*Les Enfants du paradis*), plays Berlioz. Produced by the Nazi-controlled studio, Continental, the film was severely criticized by Goebbels for its patriotic glorification of French art and was not permitted exhibition outside of France.

Emil Jannings (1886–1950). Eminent German actor who, prior to the talkies, starred in films of Ernst Lubitsch (*Madame Dubarry, Anne Boleyn*) and F. W. Murnau (*The Last Laugh, Faust*) as well as in Hollywood films by Victor Fleming (*The Way of All Flesh*) and Josef von Sternberg (*The Last Command*), for which he received the first Academy Award for best performance. In 1940 he was appointed the head of UFA studio by the Nazis and was blacklisted after the war. *Le President Krüger*, directed by Hans Steinhoff, was a 1940 propaganda film.

Bel Ami. An Austrian film (1939), directed by Willi Forst.

3. Théâtre Montmartre. The name of the theater is invented.
4. Grand Guignol is a subgenre of melodrama. Horror and spectacular scenic effects (with particular emphasis on violence and disfigurement) are its dominant characteristics. The Théâtre du Grand Guignol became the home of this style.
5. *Le Père Goriot.* Film version (not released until 1944) of Balzac's celebrated novel, directed by Robert Vernay, with a script by Charles Spaak.

Billancourt. The Billancourt studio was one of the prominent French film production facilities. (The interior sequences of several of Jean Renoir's films of the 1930s, for example, were shot there.)

6. Daxiat. The character Daxiat is modeled on Alain Laubreaux, the notorious pro-Nazi critic whose work appeared in *Je suis partout* (see note 8, below). Laubreaux, in fact, used the pseudonym "Daxiat" for certain of his own writings, including a play. (Truffaut has said that Daxiat was also suggested in part by another actual figure, a "talented filmmaker," but he has provided no further identification.)

7. *Britannicus.* Title of a tragedy by the neoclassical French playwright Jean Racine, first performed in 1669. Some interpretations of the play have been based in part on the possibility of sexual attraction of the emperor Nero—at the very beginning of his cruel reign—for the young Roman Britannicus.

8. *Je suis partout* (literally *I Am Everywhere*). A French newspaper noted for its extreme rightist positions before the war and, during the Occupation, for its virulently anti-Semitic polemics.

9. *Jew Süss* (*Jud Süss*). A German film of 1940, directed by Veit Harlan, with a screenplay by Thea von Harbou and starring Emil Jannings. The most rabidly anti-Semitic of the several screen versions of this traditional story, *Jud Süss* is the paradigmatic expression of Nazi racial views.

10. Comédie Française. The French national theater company, founded in 1658 and traditionally devoted above all to the performance of major classical French drama.

11. Sacha Guitry (1885–1957). A prolific actor-director-writer-producer who, in 1942, staged his 114th play. His film *Give Me Your Eyes* (1943) is recalled by Truffaut as "the only film to give a true account of the reality of the blackout." Moreover, according to Truffaut, Jean-Loup's series of arrests (see shots 599 and 600) echo Guitry's difficulties with the authorities after the Liberation.

12. *Mehr licht.* "More light," the last words of the great German poet and playwright Johann Wolfgang von Goethe (1749–1832).

13. Jean Gabin. The most popular actor in the history of French cinema, Jean Gabin played the role of the strong but gentle railroad engineer subject to inexplicable fits of violent jealousy in Jean Renoir's film version (1938) of Emile Zola's naturalist novel *The Human Beast* (*La Bête humaine*).

14. *The Dead Queen* (*La Reine morte*). The first play of novelist Henri de Montherlant, *La Reine morte* was produced with great success at the Comédie Française in 1942, marking the beginning of Montherlant's prolific theatrical activity.

15. Jean Yonnel. French stage actor who appeared in the first production of *La Reine morte*. Denounced as a Romanian Jew by Alain Laubreaux (see note 6 above), Yonnel denied the accusation.

16. This law was enacted on 6 June 1942.

17. Pitoëff. Celebrated theatrical family. Georges (1884–1939) emigrated from Russia to France and founded a repertory theater. His son, Sacha (born 1920), continued the family tradition, specializing in the plays of Chekhov, Gorky, and Ibsen. His most

significant screen performance is as "M" in Alain Resnais's *Last Year at Marienbad* (*L'Année dernière à Marienbad*, 1961).

18. *The Hairy Ape* (1922) is a play by the American dramatist Eugene O'Neill.

19. *Deux gaules*, French for two fishing rods, is very close in sound to "de Gaulle," that is, General Charles de Gaulle (1890–1970), exiled leader of the anti-Nazi resistance (and later president of France, 1945–1946 and 1959–1969).

20. The full range of Parisian theatrical activity is suggested by the contrast between the music halls of the working-class neighborhood of Ménilmontant and the Théâtre National de l'Opéra.

21. Edith Piaf was the most celebrated French woman singer of her time (1915–1963). The "theme song" of *The Last Metro* ("Mon Amant de Saint-Jean") carries clear echoes of the Piaf style.

22. Sacré-Coeur. The Basilica of the Sacred Heart, which dominates many views in the Montmartre section of Paris.

23. Colonial Exposition. It is not clear which exposition is alluded to here. There were numerous expositions—universal, international, colonial—held in Europe during the first third of the century. The three major French colonial expositions were organized in Marseilles (1906 and 1922) and in Vincennes, a suburb of Paris (1931), and were essentially exhibitions of the products of the French colonies.

24. *Boches*. A long-standing French term of hostility for the Germans, especially German soldiers.

25. *A Doll's House*. A popular play of the Norwegian dramatist Henrik Ibsen (1828–1906). Marion presumably played Nora.

26. Between shots 281 and 282, and then between 283 and 284, there exists a six-minute sequence deleted from all theatrical release prints of *The Last Metro* but included in the video cassette of the film available in France. Since the sequence exists only, to our knowledge, on the French videotape, and since Truffaut agreed to its exclusion from theatrical prints, we will provide only a summary.

In the first segment (following 281), the playwright Valentin, from whom Marion earlier received a script in her hotel lobby (see 88), arrives at the Théâtre Montmartre. He speaks briefly with Arlette, invoking his memories of happier times in this theater. Germaine then leads him up to Marion's office. In the second segment, Marion compliments Valentin warmly on the script, entitled *The Angels of Mercy*. Valentin tells her that he wrote it with her in mind for the principal role of Sister Saint-Jean. Marion replies that she cannot play the role, having promised Lucas to devote herself to his theater during his absence. When Marion expresses the hope that when she does return to the screen it will be in a film written by Valentin, he replies that *The Angels of Mercy* will be his last script: the doctors have told him that he does not have long to live. As Valentin reflects on his approaching death, Marion looks through a pile of scripts on her desk for *The Angels of Mercy* in order to return it to Valentin, but she is unable to find it. Valentin tells her not to bother: "If you find it, keep it as a souvenir of me." As Valentin leaves, Marion invites him to dinner; he replies that he is leaving the next day for the mountains. And when Marion tries to kiss him good-bye, he replies that now kissing him is dangerous, and he instead raises his hand to stroke Marion's cheek.

This excised sequence is significant in two ways. First, it prepares us for the allusion to *The Angels of Mercy* in the nightclub sequence below (see 298 to 302) and heightens the irony of the description of the filming of *The Angels of Mercy* during the last days of the war (see 573 and 574) with Nadine now playing the role written for Marion (the film is presumably made from the script that Valentin leaves in Marion's office). Second, this sequence suggests that the character of Valentin is based at least in part on the eminent playwright Jean Giraudoux (1882–1944), who is given dialogue credit for Robert Bresson's first feature film, *The Angels of Sin*, a film about nuns to which the title *Angels of Mercy* clearly alludes. (Truffaut has adjusted the dates somewhat: the Bresson film, though indeed made during the Occupation, was filmed in 1943, not near the end of the war as is *The Angels of Mercy*, and its appearance predated the death of Giraudoux.)

This sequence is reproduced in its entirety in the issue of *L'Avant-Scène Cinéma* on *The Last Metro*, pages 84–85.

27. Galeries Lafayette. A Paris department store, one of the largest in the world.

28. Presumably the Nazis were unaware that this song—the title means "To me you are beautiful"—was written for a Yiddish-speaking and not a German-speaking public.

29. *School for Wives* (*L'Ecole des femmes*). The first (1662) of the great comedies by the neoclassical French playwright Molière. In this play, the very young Agnès is brought up in total innocence by her guardian Arnolphe.

30. Marshal Henri Philippe Pétain (1856–1951) was premier of the French government at Vichy (1940–1944) and was convicted of treason in 1945.

31. For the background of this episode, see Marais, "Confronting a Critic," in this volume.

32. *The Magic Mountain* (*Der Zauberberg*, 1924). Perhaps the most famous work of the German novelist Thomas Mann.

33. FFI (French Forces of the Interior). Underground paramilitary forces, united under a single command beginning in 1943. These guerrilla units were effective in the Resistance, particularly in railroad sabotage, and in coordinating with the Allied campaign in 1944. They also played a role in the prosecution of collaborators after the Liberation.

Contexts

A Letter to the Crew of *The Last Metro*

François Truffaut

The following letter was addressed to the crew by the director just before shooting began on *The Last Metro*. It reveals at least two significant aspects of Truffaut's working style. First, the salutation, "My Dear Friends"—a salutation which in Truffaut's voice asks to be taken literally—proclaims Truffaut's sense of those qualities that the shooting of a Truffaut film shared with a gathering of friends, qualities fully dramatized in his own film about filmmaking, *Day for Night* (1973). Second, by announcing that the set would be closed to journalists, the letter reminds us of the place of *The Last Metro* in Truffaut's career. One might say, without meaning to establish rigid categories, that Truffaut had long alternated works of an idiosyncratic and experimental nature with works aimed at the larger movie-going public. Truffaut told interviewers that he needed at least one commercial success in every three pictures in order to keep his career going, but before *The Last Metro* he had not enjoyed that kind of success since *The Story of Adele H.* (1975), five years and four films earlier. By closing the set of *The Last Metro*, perhaps Truffaut sought to pique public curiosity about the film, a curiosity already aroused by his collaboration for the first time in years with big-name stars, in this case two of the most popular in France, Catherine Deneuve and Gérard Depardieu.

January 21, 1980

My Dear Friends,

We are about to shoot a film together.

Before beginning, we all have stage fright, that is to say, our imaginations embrace and build upon unsubstantial anxieties. It may seem to us now that our *previous* experience will be of no use *this time*, and that the making of *The Last Metro* hides pernicious obstacles we've never faced before.

But not at all. I think that *The Last Metro* will be an easy and pleasant movie to shoot, as is always the case when the characters are more important than the situations. In short, in my opinion, only the film should get all wound up.

In any case, we must have all had a really oppressive education to find ourselves plagued by such systematic doubts about our own ability in this, one of those rare occupations that is also a calling, one that allows the element of pleasure to occupy a front-row seat.

Now, then, let's forget our stage fright, let's imagine that we are all making our way through *The Last Metro* like fish through water.

We are going to work with the purpose of telling an interesting and intriguing story. I propose that we keep this story a secret, and that we avoid telling it to the press. Let's even avoid describing the characters. What happens in the Théâtre Montmartre, from the cellar to the attic, concerns just us and . . . the audience with which we have a date—but not until nine months from now (by necessity).

The camera crew, under the direction of Nestor Almendros, will do its best to create beautiful images, to evoke the period of the Occupation with accuracy. Let's not allow the haphazard intrusions of TV news cameras to give a confused picture of our work.

Without offending our colleagues from the press and from television, without going so far as to compete for any prizes for lack of cooperation, let's delay until the fall season all so-called promotional activities—that is until the moment when, under strict control, these activities can be helpful in launching the film to the public.

Knowing that each of you will be approached separately by the media, I thought it might be easier for you to decline if it is established from this moment forward that the set of *The Last Metro* is closed to journalists. . . .

And now, let this filming be a party, and let the party begin.

Best,

François Truffaut

Interview with
François Truffaut

Annette Insdorf

A somewhat different version of Annette Insdorf's interview with François Truffaut appeared in the *New York Times* (8 February 1981, sec. 2, pp. 21 and 28) on the eve of the theatrical release of *The Last Metro* under the title "How Truffaut's 'The Last Metro' Reflects Occupied Paris."

Annette Insdorf, an associate professor at Yale and Columbia, is the author of *François Truffaut* and *Indelible Shadows: Film and the Holocaust*. She is a frequent contributor to the *New York Times* Arts and Leisure section.

François Truffaut's *The Last Metro* rode triumphantly into New York, following a standing ovation at the closing night of the New York Film Festival. In France, it has been the most popular hit for the director of *The 400 Blows*, *Jules and Jim*, and *Day for Night*. "A dazzlingly subversive work," declared Vincent Canby about this affectionate exploration of a Parisian theater company during the German occupation.

When Lucas Steiner (Heinz Bennent), a German-Jewish stage director, is forced to go underground in 1942, his wife, Marion (Catherine Deneuve), takes over their theater with a firm hand. Her young leading man, Bernard Granger (Gérard Depardieu), is torn between joining the Resistance and enacting a more subtle resistance (remaining on stage)—to the charms of Marion and to compromise with the pro-Nazi critic Daxiat (Jean-Louis Richard). The limitations of war

define the possibilities of theater as the troupe gets the play up and the curtain down in time for the last metro before curfew.

The prolific Truffaut spoke in New York about the genesis of his latest work, commented on its muted but unflinching depiction of anti-Semitism, and reassessed the concept of the director as *auteur*.

The forty-eight-year-old filmmaker had felt the rumblings of *The Last Metro* for some time. "I always thought of making this film," he revealed between gulps of espresso. "At the beginning of my career, I couldn't do it because it was too close to *The 400 Blows*—not in terms of the Occupation, but my own age at that time. Then I thought of doing a love story about the Occupation, but when I saw *The Sorrow and the Pity*, I said to myself, 'How can I make a fiction film about the period that could measure up to *The Sorrow and the Pity?!*'

"Then, of course, the subject came into vogue and there was a whole series of French films about the Occupation—like *Lacombe Lucien*, *Les Violons du bal*, and *Mr. Klein*. So I said again, 'This is not the right moment.'" After the wave subsided, Truffaut was stimulated by actor Jean Marais's autobiography—as well as by other documents by and about theater people during the Occupation.

Actors' memoirs, meticulous research, and the director's own experiences as a child in wartime France provided the abundant details that punctuate *The Last Metro*. "The script is nourished by real things," explained Truffaut. "It shows the resourcefulness and ruses of daily life during the Occupation. War films usually have big events and heroic actions; *The Last Metro* is interesting, I suppose, because of its small details. It's almost as if seen by a child because the things that struck me at the time are woven into the film." Of equal importance for Truffaut is the contribution of co-scenarist and assistant director Suzanne Schiffman, who was also approximately ten at the time. "She brought in more dramatic elements. After all, her mother was deported and never came back," he added.

While Truffaut's wartime experiences were less traumatizing, the deportation of his uncle to a small concentration camp (because of politics rather than religion) feeds into *The Last Metro*. On the day of his arrest, this uncle prevented a Resistance comrade from suffering a similar fate by quietly signaling *not* to acknowledge him at their rendezvous. "We simply transposed the locale from a train station to a church," said the director about the scene of Bernard's close call with the Gestapo.

Truffaut recalled the Occupation as a period when "everything was paradoxical. We were told to be honest, while surrounded by examples of the dishonesty needed to survive. For example, without food tickets, we would have starved. We had false tickets—badly made, obviously—so children were sent to the grocer's: 'They'll close their eyes and wouldn't dare send back kids,' we said. I'm sure that my profound wariness of all certitudes stems from this period."

Truffaut admitted that "had *The Last Metro*—which is not easily categorizable—come out a few years ago, it would have been attacked for being very tolerant of the characters and expressing sympathy for everyone, including those 'show people' who continued to perform during the war. But now," he added from behind a cloud of cigar smoke, "since Mao's death, the invasion of Afghanistan, and the upheaval in Iran, it's once again possible to accept the idea that life is paradoxical."

His vision of filmmaking is a far cry from the didactic social commentary that has characterized much of European cinema: "After '68, in Europe, there was an excessive politicization of life: politics were overestimated. You kept hearing the slogan 'everything is political'—which I find absurd."

In *The Last Metro*, this line is uttered by the Nazi sympathizer Daxiat (based on an actual critic of the extreme right) as a justification for running the Jews out of France. One of the few villains in Truffaut's sympathetic body of work, this character illustrates the filmmaker's premise that there was often more to fear from the pro-Nazi French than from the Germans.

"That's why there are almost no Germans in the film. One of the most monstrous things during the war was the 'Rafle du Vél'd'hiv,' and it was the French who did it,'' he elaborated, referring to the roundup of 13,000 Jews by the Paris police on July 16, 1942. (This event, which facilitated neat deportation to concentration camps from Paris's Vélodrome d'Hiver, is also reconstructed in Joseph Losey's *Mr. Klein*.)

With his dark eyes darting quickly, Truffaut recounted a story about the roundup that struck him as particularly horrific: "Someone phoned the police and said, 'They told us what to do with men, women, and children, but no one told us what to do with the animals.' The response was, 'Give the pets to the concierges.' So the dogs and cats were saved this way. Crazy, non?" he asked quietly.

Despite *The Last Metro*'s sensitivity to the plight of Jews in wartime France, anti-Semitism is hardly its main theme. While the film calls attention to the fact that actors had to have an Aryan Certificate in order to act on stage or screen, it does not dwell, for example, on the point that Jews had to ride in the last car of the train. Truffaut's contention that "this film is not concerned merely with anti-Semitism but intolerance in general" is evidenced by *The Last Metro*'s comfortable accommodation of a gay director (Jean Poiret) and a lesbian designer (Andréa Ferréol).

Why include these nonproblematic characterizations? "Suzanne and I observed that the collaborationist, extreme-right press condemned Jews and homosexuals in the same breath. The French pro-Nazis had a very naive image of Germany—virile male strength. It's absurd to look only at films like Visconti's *The Damned*: sure, there were lots of homosexuals in the SS. But for the Nazis, the weak were 'female' in a pejorative sense. Hence, the phobia against homosexuals. It always pops up in reviews of the collaborationist newspaper *Je suis partout* [I Am Everywhere]. You read, for instance, 'A play that reeks of Jewishness and effeminacy.'"

In *The Last Metro*, this accusation is leveled by Daxiat at the Steiner productions. The role of Lucas Steiner—a Jew who is clearly not effeminate—was in fact a source of tension when it was first given to Bennent. Over dinner in Paris six months ago, Truffaut voiced doubts about casting a German actor (who had just incarnated an eager Nazi in *The Tin Drum*) as a Jew. Once the film opened, he admitted, "Suzanne felt that only a Jewish actor could play a Jew. But it's one of those problems that one creates for oneself. Bennent is a great actor, and I'm no longer afraid that he won't be plausible as a Jew—even in Germany. In France, no one recognizes him from Schlöndorff's films. They simply ask, 'Who's this great actor?'"

The role of Lucas Steiner took shape from speculation about a celebrated French performer: "The Germans wanted Louis Jouvet to stay in France and stage German plays. But Jouvet took his troupe to Portugal and then South America. Our point of departure was, what if Jouvet had remained, hidden in the cellar of his theater?"

Bennent's scenes are appropriately dark—literally and figuratively. As the uncomprehending victim of a racial hatred that takes no account of the individual, he is almost never in the light. "There is no sunshine in the film," added the director. "Visually, Nestor [Almendros, the cinematographer] and I made a great effort not to have day scenes until fifty minutes into the film. You feel more in the period when it's nocturnal." They also decided to use Fuji rather than Kodak film because "it affords more depth, especially in night scenes," he pointed out.

The visual texture extends into the tone of *The Last Metro*, for even the comic moments are quite somber. Truffaut defined the style as "dramatic comedy—a particularly French tone," and he disagreed with comparisons that have been made between his film and *To Be or Not to Be*, Ernst Lubitsch's black comedy of 1942. "I don't think you can make farces today," he insisted. "Well, maybe Mel Brooks can. But not the French. And it would be ridiculous to remake *To Be or Not to Be*."

For this critic-turned-filmmaker, the whole question of influence and *hommage* has become something of a bad joke. "The cinema has suffered lately from the films of cinephiles," he declared. "Sometimes viewers place too much importance on what they think is quotation from another film. Influences are ancient rather than recent—an impregnation. I don't want to make films of quotations. *The Last Metro* is my nineteenth film: I think more about what I lost or did well in the previous eighteen than about other people's work," he maintained.

Moreover, the critic whose provocative articles for *Cahiers du cinéma* in the 1950s helped create the cult of the *auteur* now finds that the director needs to be demythologized. "There's an entire vocabulary that has to be abandoned, like 'direction of actors.' As a director, I'm ashamed of this phrase. I struggle against the very word—I *direct* no one. I'm not a captain! I point them toward what is good for them or for the film.

"When you switch from critic to filmmaker," he continued with growing intensity, "you can't use the same expressions—and certainly not *cinéma d'auteur*. The terms you could manipulate as a critic become shocking in the mouth of a director. Take *hommage*, for example: now you can copy anything, plagiarize, and call it homage. We have to stop talking of these things. Influence is a question of spirit, not quotation."

For Truffaut, the scene in which Marion knocks her husband down (to keep him from surrendering to the Gestapo) constitutes a more profound debt to film history than *The Last Metro*'s thematic link to Lubitsch or Jean Renoir. He revealed that the scene "as written had become too heavy with interminable dialogue. We said to ourselves, 'what would they have done in the silent cinema? Before 1930, she would have hit him on the head!' This liberated us. And this is one of my preoccupations: why did the directors of silent films take their secrets with them? Why is our cinema less and less alive? Even talkies made by directors who began in the silent era are unique: they adopt radical solutions that wouldn't strike someone who began after 1930."

Truffaut was amused by the question put to Deneuve at the New York Film Festival press conference, "Why does Marion then slap Bernard?" The idea of motivation never occurred to either the director or the actress; rather, "We wrote it as a gag, but in Cocteau's sense of a tragic gag—it's not to make you laugh. Her slap is a bit like Nelly Borgeaud's sudden actions in *The Man Who Loved Women*. Or like my mother who was violent and unpredictable. Catherine never asked, 'Why a slap?' But in America, this would have been discussed at each stage of the film's development!"

In Truffaut's opinion, Americans have a stronger sense of concept than the French. As an example, he proposed that if a French director were to recount the story of his next film, "he would tell it as if it had never been told before, since the beginning of cinema history. An American director would simply answer the questions, 'who are the actors?, what is the background?', as if it's understood that it's always the same story, only the background changes," he added with a laugh.

Despite his starring role in Steven Spielberg's *Close Encounters of the Third Kind*, the American cinema is still unfamiliar territory for Truffaut. To the question of whether he would consider directing an American film, he responded, "The place is not important. The only question is the language—French or English. Kubrick makes American films without setting foot in America! If I had four or five properties, and one would be as logical in English as in French, I'd say maybe it could be in English. But *The Last Metro*, for example, could never have been made in English."

The notion of planning four or five projects at a time may seem like a risky juggling act, but Truffaut has always performed it nimbly. "I work in cycles, and need four or five projects," he confessed. "The order can change but it reassures me to have a few. While shooting one film, I like to take notes to serve another. Otherwise, when a film is over, you feel too drained."

Now that *The Last Metro* has immersed him in the world of the theater, would Truffaut consider directing plays? Shaking his head, he answered, "If you tell me a story—that yesterday you met a boy, for example—I see the different scales while you're talking: a two-shot here, a close-up there. I still see stories in terms of shots." With obvious affection, he added, "filmmaking is a very special discipline."

Working on
The Last Metro

Nestor Almendros

n his book of reminiscences of his career as cinematographer, *A Man with a Movie Camera* [*Un Homme à la caméra*] (Paris: Hatier Editeur, 1981, pp. 171–72), written during the filming of *The Last Metro*, Nestor Almendros has recorded some of his thoughts on the film.*

Even as I finish this book, I'm shooting my eighth film with François Truffaut, *The Last Metro*. With thirteen weeks of shooting, longer than the norm for French productions, and with stars like Catherine Deneuve and Gérard Depardieu, this film assumes a place of honor in the Truffaut canon by virtue of the importance attached to its production.

For so large-scaled a work as this, I have set myself several objectives.

In the first place, there is the problem of rendering the atmosphere of the years 1940 to 1945 through lighting. This period evokes for me personal memories modified in part by my second memory: the cinema itself. On the one hand, I recall the pallid electric light of these war years; on the other hand, I remember a reality transposed into black and white. I don't mean that a color film about the Occupation is necessarily an anachronism. It was in the age of Nazism that I was struck by the first German films in Agfacolor, Von Baky's *Munchhausen* and Veit Harlan's *The Golden City*. For *The Last Metro*, since the film is not in black and white, I want to get the color of those German films—less dazzling, gentler than the Technicolor tones of American films of the same period. To help achieve this

*The excerpt that follows was translated by E. Rubinstein.

effect, Truffaut's regular designer, Jean-Pierre Kohut-Svelko, has created nearly monochromatic décors; the costumes and objects selected are of subtly graduated, very close tones.

For this film, Truffaut decided to change his film stock, that is to say, to "change his palette." After many experiments, we opted for Fuji, made in Japan. Watching the rushes, we were delighted with the results. Straight off, we got colors different from those of our earlier films and corresponding to the "memory" effect we were after.

The story of *The Last Metro* unfolds on two levels, that of the life and work of a theatrical company and that of the performance of a play. I must therefore use two different lighting systems, the first realistic and indicative of the daily life of the backstage of a theater, the other, for the scenes of the theatrical performances, deliberately artificial and stylized. These two methods of lighting allow me to use soft lights, according to the usual practice, and also, for the theatrical lighting effects, directional Frenel lamps so as to get distinct shadows, as in older films. Thanks to the basic device of the screenplay, I can make shameless use of those notorious lamps that I criticized in my youth. For the color, the effect of using expressionistic-toned gelatins on the bulbs of the footlights delivered the strange gleam that gives the faces of the actors that theatrical look.

Confronting a Critic

Jean Marais

The popular stage and film actor Jean Marais was for many years the colleague and companion of the playwright/artist/filmmaker Jean Cocteau (1889–1963).* In *Histoires de ma vie* (Stories of My Life) (Paris: Albin Michel, 1975, pp. 223–26), Marais gives his version of an actual, celebrated episode that provided the source for the sequence in *The Last Metro* in which Bernard Granger assaults Daxiat in a restaurant. The excerpts that follow also reveal the source of several other details of the film. Daxiat's attacks on Jean-Loup for his homosexuality, for example, mirror Alain Laubreaux/Daxiat's attacks on Cocteau, and the censors' suppression of a scene showing an epileptic fit in Cocteau's *The Typewriter* prefigures the suppression of a similar scene from *The Vanished One* (see shots 72 and 73 above).

A few days before opening night [of *The Typewriter* at the Théâtre Hébertot], a journalist from *Le Petit Parisien* informed me that Alain Laubreaux, critic for both that paper and *Je suis partout* and a veritable *Führer* of dramatic literature, was getting ready to "tear Cocteau to pieces."

"He hasn't seen or read the play," I said.

"That's true; just the same, his mind is made up."

"Well, you can tell Laubreaux that if he goes through with it, I'll bash his face in."

*This excerpt from *Histoires de ma vie*, by Jean Marais, was translated by E. Rubinstein.

At that time, you could only put on a play with the authorization of the German censors; in principle, this presented no problem if the play in question was not political. Hébertot had normally gotten the required permit. The day after the dress rehearsal—which, for once, had gone without incident—the production was banned. Hébertot went off to the Germans and pointed out the inconsistency of their ban. They answered, "That's logical enough: so we either have to reimburse all your expenses or authorize the production."

Two days later, the performances were allowed on condition that we suppress the epileptic fit at the end of the second act. The German censors were trying to save face.

Alain Laubreaux didn't show up. Nonetheless, what a vicious review! Not content with tearing the play and the actors to shreds, he indulged in vile attacks both on Cocteau's writing and on his private life. I was obliged to live up to my word: whatever the price, I had to strike.

. . . We dined every night after the show at a little restaurant nearby. . . . One hot and menacing spring evening, I was having supper with Cocteau and Michèle Alfa when I was advised that Hébertot wanted to see me. He was in a private diningroom on the second floor. I went up. The storm had broken out. The windows of the room were open, the lights turned off because of the blackout. Outside, it was coming down in buckets: lightning, thunder, a night out of Shakespeare. At first, I didn't see a thing. In the glimmer of the lightning bolts, I recognized Hébertot's bald skull. I held out my hand to him. Then I noticed another member of the party, someone I knew, and I greeted him. Then someone else, to whom I introduced myself. He didn't give his name. Hébertot said to me "That's Alain Laubreaux."

"It can't be true!" I said.

"Yes, it's Alain Laubreaux!"

"If it is, I'll spit in his face. Sir, are you Alain Laubreaux?"

He didn't answer. I repeated, "Sir, are you Alain Laubreaux?"

He said yes. And I spit. He got up. I thought he wanted to fight. I hit him.

The little restaurateur, who had followed me, separated us: "Not in my restaurant! Not in my restaurant!" . . .

"Okay," I said, "I'll go outside to bash his face in."

I went down the stairs. The members of my party on the ground floor begged me to be careful.

"Laubreaux is with the Gestapo," Jean said to me. "We'll be shot."

"This is not your affair," I answered. "I don't think he's with the Gestapo, but anyhow I said I'd smash his face in and I will. . . ."

I wait for more than a quarter hour. He doesn't come down. At last I see him, followed by Hébertot and the other fellow. They leave the restaurant. I follow them. It's still raining buckets.

Laubreaux has a big square cane. I grab it from him. If I use the cane on him, I run the risk of killing him. I toss the cane to the other side of the Boulevard des Batignolles. I attack Laubreaux with my fists. He falls. His brow is cut open. He screams, "Help! Police!" I can't take any credit: he didn't defend himself. And I continue to pummel him, in time with my cries, rhythmically: "And Jean-Louis Barrault? What did he ever do to you? And Bertheau? And Bourdet?"

In my crazed litany, I invoke all his victims. Then I go back into the restaurant. Someone offers me a glass of champagne. Laubreaux comes back to call the police emergency number. Fortunately, the little restaurateur has cut off the line.

And Jean and I went home in the pelting rain.

A Sampling of Reviews

A Sampling of Reviews

New York Times
Vincent Canby

François Truffaut's "The Last Metro" is a dazzlingly subversive work. . . . Not since Lubitsch's "To Be or Not to Be" has there been such a triumphantly unorthodox use of grim material that usually prompts movies of pious, prefabricated responses. . . .

"The Last Metro" doesn't dwell on the horrors of Nazi-encouraged, French anti-Semitism, which flourished during the occupation, but it is haunted by those horrors. They are there in the sorrowful love scenes of Marion and Lucas Steiner, which are among the loveliest moments in all of Mr. Truffaut's works, and in what seem to be throwaway scenes. . . .

The movie, which was photographed by Nestor Almendros, even looks haunted and a bit hungry. The colors are mostly muted. The streets of Paris have the cramped look of streets shot in a studio, which recalls the look of films of 40 years ago and reflects the feeling of restriction of life in an occupied zone.

. . . I'd also like to commend the shape of the film, which effectively covers the two years of the occupation and leads to a conclusion that, for sheer, bold theatricality, may remind you of the end of Luis Buñuel's "Tristana."

"Tristana" doesn't pop into the mind by chance. It's not since "Tristana" that Miss Deneuve has had a role to match that of Marion Steiner. . . .

It takes a little while to catch the tempo of the film, but pay attention. "The Last Metro" is about lives surrounded by melodrama, being lived with as little outward fuss as possible.·. . .

(12 October 1980, p. 71)

Wall Street Journal
Joy Gould Boyum

All this [the predictable "happy ending" and the "neat" division of characters into "good and bad"] makes for a comforting and comfortable vision: of life, of the theater, of the occupation. And it's a view very tempting to go along with—particularly for the French. After all, this is the first film in years in which they have emerged not as a nation of collaborators but of heroes and resisters.

Still, this vision ends up seeming less innocent and simple than naive and simplistic. The characters we meet are viewed totally from the outside and not because the film is being meaningfully reticent about them: It seems to have no comprehension of the nature of their emotions. We are distanced from any grasp of what is going on within the characters. . . .

As for the theater, which during the occupation managed to thrive and play a politically significant role . . . , what we are shown seems incredibly superficial. To say that the theater provides an escape and a ref-

uge is really not to say anything very special. . . .

(20 February 1981, p. 29)

Boston Phoenix
David Chute

. . . But if the film's contention that these muffled lives and tentative relationships are in fact heroic lends some thematic cohesion, it doesn't make the people any more satisfying to watch. *The Last Metro* feels amorphous and half-formed; Truffaut's conception has remained as foggy as the dank semitwilight shrouding Paris. In the way he keeps the history-laden story flowing along, so that each fact-based incident settles gently into place, he is firmly in control. Yet both the style and the characters seem to owe as much to early generations of romantic movie characters as to his own intuitions. He loves these people, but his love is an oddly incurious one. . . . The French, understandably, have made *The Last Metro* Truffaut's most financially successful film, and have showered it with prestigious awards— an appropriate outcome, since the slightly stiff, almost anachronistic staging seems a throwback to the handsomely mounted films of the Gallic Tradition of Quality—which the New Wave supposedly rejected.

(24 February 1981, sec. 3, p. 4)

Variety
"Len"

François Truffaut's 19th feature is his richest, most satisfying film in years, and could earn him the joint critical-commercial success that has been eluding him of late. . . .

Truffaut . . . has successfully wrestled with a mountain of factual material and compressed it into a memorable gallery of composite personages and incidents. The first part of the film threatens to sacrifice character to anecdote, but once it finds its equilibrium, the narrative flows smoothly, with its full weight of emotion.

Truffaut's direction is uncharacteristically restrained, his mise-en-scène almost classical in its invisible camerawork and sober editing. Inevitably, he indulges his penchant for filmic references . . . but rarely have they seemed more appropriate.

(17 September 1980, p. 18)

Cineaste
Peter Pappas

The film's center of gravity is the collectivity of the theater company; however, it is a center that will not hold. The problem is that Truffaut, as in all of his work, is not interested in collectives but in individuals. Thus, the massive nature of the . . . holocaust . . . is reduced to the private level of a domestic tragedy. . . . Before

everything else, fascism destroyed humanity's sense of individual fate; one could no longer claim that life—or death—were either lonely or discrete.

But in *The Last Metro*, there is no community of despair, only a vague commonality of several separate desperations. . . . In the end, the film is not so much about a last metro of common travail as it is about a last hurrah of professional success. The Steiner company triumphs because it refuses to join the collective struggle, separating itself from it and denying its priority. . . .

Nevertheless . . . Truffaut's film contains a number of small, and several substantial, pleasures. The small pleasures all lie in the mise-en-scène. Truffaut's camera movements and extended (but not long) takes are so clean and precise as to be absolutely classical (in fact, the scenes shot in the street where the Steiner theater is located remind one of a "purified" Renoir). In this time of visual illiteracy and incompetence, to see a film that is intelligently—and correctly—composed is to behold a small wonder.

(vol. 10, no. 4, Fall 1980, pp. 9–11)

The Village Voice
Andrew Sarris

Truffaut himself never professed to be a "political" filmmaker per se. At the time of the Algerian war he stated in an interview that the only comment he could make on the conflict was contained in *Shoot the Piano Player*, a portrait of a character paralyzed by his reluctance to make moral commitments. In this respect, *The Last Metro* reflects a certain degree of nostalgia for a period and a genre in which the moral commitments of characters could be taken for granted. What disturbs me the most about *The Last Metro* is that the uneasy mixture of fact and fantasy is never adequately articulated into a coherent whole. Truffaut is trying to establish connections between theater and politics, between personal relationships and political involvements, between the idealism of the few and the pragmatism of the many. The film is full of carefully planted "touches" that may seem telling to Parisians and merely quaint to New Yorkers. Early on in the film, for example, a passing German soldier pats a little French boy's head. The boy's mother drags him off for a politically purifying shampoo. . . . There is more to Truffaut's ritual . . . than the ceremonial shampoo. There is also the German's original gesture, a disconcertingly kindly intimation of a shared humanity between the conqueror and the vanquished. Jean Renoir's cinematic hymns to Franco-German camaraderie after both World War I (*La Grande Illusion*) and World War II (*The Elusive Corporal*) are, of

course, very close to Truffaut's heart and artistic soul. . . .

Truffaut's characters in *The Last Metro* are not, by and large, obsessed ideologues. Even the members of the Resistance among them seem to be driven more by theatrical narcissism than by philosophical conviction. . . . Yet if the politics remain muffled and subterranean, both literally and figuratively, the theatrics never take off to the loftier realms of a *Les Enfants du Paradis* or *Golden Coach*. . . .

. . . Truffaut himself has gone into extensive rhetorical detail on the absurdities and cruelties of anti-Semitism and homophobia. Most of this rhetoric is hurled at the film's arch-villain. . . . The Daxiat character strikes me as too convenient a diabolical device to concentrate all the poisons of an era into one thoroughly discredited personality. Daxiat makes it much too easy for a self-congratulatory euphoria to settle over the audience.

I do not want to be too hard on *The Last Metro*. That it will be one of the better films of 1981 goes almost without saying. . . .

(11 February 1981, pp. 47, 54)

New York Times
Janet Maslin

Mr. Truffaut is at his very best with "The Last Metro," which has a grim setting but becomes as much of a comedy as it is a love story and World War II drama. . . .

"The Last Metro" is a work of exceptional precision, even for Mr. Truffaut. And it achieves that precision obliquely, through elegant understatement, using methods that might not ordinarily lend themselves to clarity. . . . Emotions are carefully controlled, thoughts are expressed indirectly, everything is kept carefully under wraps. The performers . . . are more impressive for what they don't do than for what they do.

. . . The camera knows more about the characters than they know about themselves. . . .

[The] reds and golds [of the nightclub setting are] too rich for the rest of the film [and the] soothing peach-colored scenery on the stage [during the Gestapo agents' visit] contrasts with the staccato pace of the editing. The look of "The Last Metro" is handsome and placid, but that in itself becomes a source of tension. The film offers a constant invitation to question the way things appear.

(19 October 1980, sec. 2, pp. 1, 19)

L'Express*
Michel Delain

You can touch the flats, breathe the dust backstage; you shiver from the humidity, tense at the inquisitional approach of Daxiat. . . .

. . . At the conclusion of *The Last Metro*, when the screen goes dark, you want to applaud, just as you do at the theater.

(27 September 1980, p. 18)

Le Monde
Jacques Siclier

Why [did Truffaut choose] the theater rather than the cinema? Because that's where performance—comedy or drama—blends most thoroughly with real life as Jean Renoir had often demonstrated. Renoir had extracted from this precept a philosophy for his own films. This [*The Last Metro*] is Truffaut's *Golden Coach*, beautiful, free in tone, deriving true joy, deep pleasure from a serious subject. It is a meditation on "Where is theater? where is life?" in which a stunning Catherine Deneuve is chiefly responsible for controlling the action. She reveals herself through the challenge of this role as Anna Magnani [as Camilla in *The Golden Coach*] had before her. . . .

In order to sustain his gamelike mise-en-scène, Truffaut has recreated Paris as it might have been portrayed in a 1940s film, a studio version of Paris, limited to the locations necessary to the action.

The very color—which was not current at the time except in the first German Agfacolor movies—appears to be an interpretation of black and white designed to suggest past time, night and fog, lowered lights, weather somewhere between blustery and stormy. (Nestor Almendros has done an admirable job.)

. . . Truffaut is less interested in the political or sociological weight of history than in its mythologies, laden as they are with memory and intrigue. Since his subject is the theater—the performance—he cultivates the distancing effects of cinematic illusion through artifice and stylization, all the while remaining interested in those events that influence man's destiny. Here, the events in question are the consequence of war and German occupation on a milieu threatened by the racial and Fascist laws of collaboration.

(18 September 1980, p. 19)

Cahiers du cinéma
Yann Lardeau

There will be those who reproach François Truffaut for his overly optimistic, too rosy portrait of the Occupation. But, if *The Last Metro* misleads us at all, it is due only to its unkept promises, its false suspense. The plot unfolds as if Truffaut had

been unable to weave all the dramatic devices he assembled into a single action (the survival of the theater, Steiner's escape). There are shots that serve only to supply a purely decorative reference to a historical moment—a use that falls far short of exploiting their true value. Is this the unfortunate effect of an inevitable compromise? . . . These scenes—exteriors for the most part—demonstrate the great danger that hovers over the Théâtre Montmartre; they contain strong indications of suspicious behavior on the part of the characters and the certainty that some eye will see. . . . And yet they have no consequence. By reminding us that what is essential takes place in the theater, the growing of tobacco, the Sunday painter, the everyday occurrences in the street outside, these humorous touches are increasingly consonant with the spirit of the film. The audience applauds Deneuve, Depardieu and Bennent. This tragicomedy is the film.

(October 1980, no. 316, p. 20)

*French reviews translated by Mirella Jona Affron.

Filmography
Bibliography

Truffaut Filmography, 1957–1983

1957 *Les Mistons* (*The Mischief-Makers*)
Screenplay: François Truffaut
Based on a short story in *Virginales* by Maurice Pons

1958 *Une Histoire d'eau* (*A Water Story*)
Co-direction: Jean-Luc Godard
Screenplay: Jean-Luc Godard

1959 *Les Quatre Cents Coups* (*The 400 Blows*)
Screenplay: François Truffaut
Dialogue: Marcel Moussy
Based on the short story by François Truffaut

1960 *Tirez sur le Pianiste* (*Shoot the Piano Player*)
Screenplay: François Truffaut, Marcel Moussy
Based on the novel by David Goodis, *Down There*

1961 *Jules et Jim* (*Jules and Jim*)
Screenplay: François Truffaut, Jean Gruault
Based on the novel by Henri-Pierre Roché

1962 *Antoine et Colette* (*Antoine and Colette*), episode in the compilation film *L'Amour à vingt ans* (*Love at Twenty*)
Screenplay: François Truffaut
Dialogue: Yvon Samuel

1964 *La Peau douce* (*Soft Skin/Silken Skin*)
Screenplay: François Truffaut, Jean-Louis Richard

1966 *Fahrenheit 451*
Screenplay: François Truffaut, Jean-Louis Richard
Dialogue: David Rudkin, Helen Scott
Based on the novel by Ray Bradbury

1967 *La Mariée était en noir* (*The Bride Wore Black*)
Screenplay: François Truffaut, Jean-Louis Richard
Based on the novel by William Irish (Cornell Woolrich)

1968 *Baisers volés* (*Stolen Kisses*)
Screenplay: François Truffaut, Claude de Givray, Bernard Revon

1969 *La Sirène du Mississippi* (*Mississippi Mermaid*)
Screenplay: François Truffaut
Based on the novel *Waltz into Darkness* by William Irish (Cornell Woolrich)

1969 *L'Enfant sauvage* (*The Wild Child*)
Screenplay: François Truffaut, Jean Gruault
Based on *Mémoire et rapport sur Victor de l'Aveyron* by Jean Itard

1970 *Domicile conjugal* (*Bed and Board*)
Screenplay: François Truffaut, Claude de Givray, Bernard Revon

1971 *Les Deux Anglaises et le continent* (*The Two English Girls*)
Screenplay: François Truffaut, Jean Gruault
Based on the novel by Henri-Pierre Roché

1972 *Une Belle Fille comme moi* (*Such a Gorgeous Kid Like Me*)
Screenplay: François Truffaut, Jean-Loup Dabadie

Based on the novel by Henry Farrell, *Such a Gorgeous Kid Like Me*

1973 *La Nuit américaine* (*Day for Night*)
Screenplay: François Truffaut, Suzanne Schiffman, Jean-Louis Richard

1975 *L'Histoire d'Adèle H.* (*The Story of Adele H.*)
Screenplay: François Truffaut, Jean Gruault, Suzanne Schiffman
Based on *Le Journal d'Adèle Hugo*

1976 *L'Argent de poche* (*Small Change*)
Screenplay: François Truffaut, Suzanne Schiffman

1977 *L'Homme qui aimait les femmes* (*The Man Who Loved Women*)
Screenplay: François Truffaut, Suzanne Schiffman, Michel Fermaud

1978 *La Chambre verte* (*The Green Room*)
Screenplay: François Truffaut, Jean Gruault
Based on "The Altar of the Dead" and "The Beast in the Jungle" by Henry James

1978 *L'Amour en fuite* (*Love on the Run*)
Screenplay: François Truffaut, Marie-France Pisier, Jean Aurel, Suzanne Schiffman

1980 *Le Dernier Métro* (*The Last Metro*)

1981 *La Femme d'à côté* (*The Woman Next Door*)
Screenplay: François Truffaut, Suzanne Schiffman, Jean Aurel

1983 *Vivement dimanche!*
(*Confidentially Yours*)

Screenplay: François Truffaut, Suzanne Schiffman, Jean Aurel
Based on the novel *The Long Saturday Night* by Charles Williams

Selected Bibliography

Walz, Eugene R. *François Truffaut: A Guide to References and Resources.* Boston: G. K. Hall, 1982. This is by far the most complete guide to works about and by Truffaut; it also includes an extensive listing of interviews.

To complement the exhaustive and definitive volume listed above, we include the following books on or by Truffaut that have appeared in English.

Allen, Don. *Truffaut.* Cinema One Series. New York: Viking, 1974.
Braudy, Leo, ed. *Focus on "Shoot the Piano Player."* Englewood Cliffs, N.J.: Prentice-Hall, 1972.
Crisp, C. G. *François Truffaut.* New York: Praeger, 1972.

Insdorf, Annette. *François Truffaut.* Boston: Twayne, 1978.
Petrie, Graham. *The Cinema of François Truffaut.* International Film Guide Series. New York: A. S. Barnes, 1970.
Truffaut, François. *The Adventures of Antoine Doinel: Four Autobiographical Screenplays.* Trans. Helen G. Scott. New York: Simon and Schuster, 1971. Includes an early treatment of *The 400 Blows*, along with the screenplays of *Antoine and Colette, Stolen Kisses*, and *Bed and Board.*
———. *Day for Night.* Trans. Sam Flores. New York: Grove Press, 1975.
———. *The Films in My Life.* Trans. Leonard Mayhew. New York: Simon and Schuster, 1978. The most

extensive collection available of Truffaut's critical pieces.

————. *The 400 Blows*. Ed. and trans. David Denby. New York: Grove Press, 1969.

————. *Hitchcock*. Trans. Helen G. Scott. New York: Simon and Schuster, 1967. Truffaut's celebrated series of interviews with one of the directors he most admires.

————. *Jules and Jim*. Trans. Nicholas Fry. New York: Simon and Schuster, 1968.

————. *The Story of Adele H*. Trans. Helen G. Scott, English dialogue by Jan Dawson. New York: Grove Press, 1976.

————. *The Wild Child*. Trans. Linda Lewin and Christine Lémery. New York: Washington Square Press, 1973.